Dreams That Help You Mourn

Lois Lindsey Hendricks

Foreword by Wayne E. Oates, PhD

Lois Hendricks

Resource Publications, Inc.
San Jose, California

Reprint Department
Resource Publications, Inc.
160 E. Virginia Street #290
San Jose, CA 95112-5876
1-408-286-8505 (voice)
1-408-287-8748 (fax)

Library of Congress Cataloging in Publication Data
Hendricks, Lois Lindsey, 1926-
 Dreams that help you mourn / Lois Lindsey Hendricks.
  p.   cm.
 Includes bibliographical references and index.
 ISBN 0-89390-395-7
 1. Death in dreams. 2. Bereavement—Psychological aspects. I. Title.
BF1099.D4H46 1997
154.6'32—dc21   97-3378

Printed in the United States of America

01 00 99 98 97 | 5 4 3 2 1

Editorial director: Nick Wagner
Editor: Kenneth Guentert
Prepress manager: Elizabeth J. Asborno
Copyeditor: Robin L. Witkin
Production assistants: Kathi Drolet, Mike Sagara, David Dunlap

In memory of Helen Kathryn, who visited me in a dream after her death and started me on my dream journey.

Contents

Part 1: Dreams Shared with Me

Crying in Dreams
The Event As It Was Recalled
The Disturbing Appearance of the Deceased Ill and Dying
Life Without the Loved One
The Spiritual Quality of Light
Mysterious Dreams and Dream-like Experiences
A Change in Daily Routine Occurs
Cremation and Interment
Delightful Dreams
Comfort Offered by Departed Loved Ones
The Management of Death and Dying
Providing Closure to Acute Grief
The Relationship of All Dreams to the Loss of a Significant Person
A Three-Year-Old's Grandfather Visits Her in Her Sleep

Part 2: Dreams Shared in Literature

Foreword

Grief or mourning may or may not occur in a specific order or stages such as shock, numbness, a struggle between fantasy and reality, depression, selective memory stirred by reminding events, bereavement dreams, and a return to the reinvestment of life in the new relationships. The occurrence of dreams about the lost loved one is the central concept of this thought-provoking book by Lois Lindsey Hendricks.

She has written this book to a wide audience of anyone concerned with their own grief or responsible for caring for bereaved persons, or anyone concerned about the variety of forms of altered states of consciousness. The human heart has reasons of which the conscious mind knows nothing. Dreams are, as Freud said, the royal road to the unconscious. Persons who have been hit by grief or professionals alike will find the book a primary source for consideration. The elaborate recording of actual dreams makes the book a source book for reflection and/or research into the nature of dreams and of grief. The book is organized around interpersonal relationships of persons grieving over the loss of parents, spouses, siblings, children, grandparents, friends, and pets. Life at its depths is about relationships and Hendricks portrays dreams as they are: a vital force in the catharsis and aberration of emotions about the loss of significant others in our lives.

I am especially intrigued by Hendricks's discussion of precognitive dreams such as clairvoyant dreams, telepathic dreams, premonitory dreams, and synchronistic dreams that occur at the same time an actual event does. These point to the mysterious nature of the human awareness and the awesome wonder that it creates in us as we watch and record the workings of the human mind.

I commend this book to you as a reader and am deeply informed by it as I think you will also be.

Wayne E. Oates, Professor of Psychiatry Emeritus
School of Medicine, University of Louisville

Preface

My interest in dreams dates back to when I was ten years old and dreamed about my little sister after her death. However, it was many years later, after having a particularly frightening dream, that I tried to understand my dreams. I attended a few workshops, which gave me even more incentive to explore my dreams individually with persons who were skilled in helping others discern the meaning of their dreams.

During that time I met Gayle Delaney while she was autographing her first book, *Living Your Dreams*, at a bookstore about two blocks from my home in San Francisco. Gayle is a clinical psychologist who works exclusively with dreams. She is the founding president of the Association for the Study of Dreams. I asked her to put my name on the list for her next dream group.

Later, while I was participating in one of her dream groups, I took the volunteer position of secretary to the Association for the Study of Dreams. At that time she was putting together the first International Conference on Dreams. Through this conference I was privileged to meet and hear important researchers, authors, and specialists on dreaming and dreams.

Since that time I have learned how much I love listening to other people's dreams and helping them to appreciate and, often, get meaning from their dreams. When I travel with my husband, who is a director of theological graduate studies and also teaches theology, I have opportunities to discuss dreams with students. These travels have taken me to Taiwan, Hong Kong, Singapore, and Malaysia. Discussing dreams with students in the medical college in Taichung, Taiwan, and being a consultant at home to a gifted high school student (who was doing her senior term paper on dreams) have been two of many rewarding experiences for me. More recently, I have been privileged to be a resource person on dreams to a research group of verbal adults at a cerebral palsy school.

Though I do not work with dreams in a clinical context, I am familiar with different approaches. Naturally, I prefer Gayle's interview technique. That is what I learned and those who tell me their dreams are comfortable with using it (see Delaney, *Living Your Dreams*, 51-58, for interview questions and *Breakthrough Dreaming* for further development of this technique).[1] I like Gayle's interview technique because it does not box dreams into a system. To force dream work into a system goes against the nature of dreams. Dreams put together all kinds of images; they mix past, present, and future time in unique ways to get your attention and to open and expand your thinking, ideas, possibilities, and options.

To appreciate the dream, even the most threatening dream, is important. Usually, talking about a frightening dream, even when it is not very well understood, gives the dreamer an appreciation for the dream. Confronting the scary figures of dreams by looking at them in conversation diminishes the fear. It is good to interact with a dream by welcoming it, loving it, and enjoying how imaginative it is, and enjoying the dream may be more important than interpreting it (Gendlin 27). Actually, many of the dreams you will read about in this book do not yield neatly

---

1 This isn't to say that others do not use similar techniques of interpreting the dream. Other techniques combine approaches to understanding dreams or use techniques in combination, adding some of their own. Two of these are Eugene T. Gendlin's *Let Your Body Interpret Your Dreams* (29-38), in which he uses sixteen questions to help the dreamer respond with a felt sense of the body, and James Gollnick's *Dreams in the Psychology of Religion*, in which he incorporates questions from several sources in the chapter "Rules for Interpreting Dreams" (134-35).

to interpretation. They may not be enjoyable either. Instead, they may help you to cry or be angry, to accept the terrible and terrifying thing that has happened in your life, and to lead you gently to return to the living. When you have allowed dreams to do that, you will, strange as it sounds, look back on them and marvel.

Since this book is also about grieving, I will include here a brief discussion about it. Grieving occurs with loss of contact evidenced by caring. The loss of contact occurs with the death of a person or a loss of a commitment in marriage, in families, in friendships, in organizations, and in institutions. Even attachments to pets, when broken by their death, their being lost, or their needing to be placed in another home, can result in grieving. An important feature of dreams is their focus on these connections with others. Montague Ullman expresses it this way: "Our dreaming self focuses on our connections to others, the intactness of those connections, and how what has happened during the day has disturbed the connections" (Ullman and Zimmerman 106). The death of someone significant in our lives can be intensely disturbing; so can a loss of commitment on the part of a spouse, family member, friend, colleague, or fellow worker.

Going back into the community as a person whose loved one is no longer alive can be a tremendous task. The role in which the deceased functioned will need to be filled. Care must be taken that new role assignments are appropriate for the age and ability of the one who is asked to assume these responsibilities. In a family each individual may grieve differently. New demands are being made and new skills are having to be learned at a time when the bereaved feels least like coping. This is true of even the youngest children, who have a more limited capacity for interpreting the cause of their painful emotions (Ullman and Zimmerman 106). The community sharing the loss—friends, acquaintances, even strangers—provide comfort from without. Martin E. Marty, theologian, says, "Through old friendships we cycle ourselves back into a story that sustains life; through new friendships we set up new stories" (*Friendship* 220). Nevertheless, the time comes, Marty reminds us, when "they have their own coffee pots to put on, their paychecks to draw, their own bright moments to celebrate" (*A Cry of Absence* 128).

After I began organizing the material I had accumulated about dream experiences of the bereaved, a book by Alan Siegel, *Dreams That Can Change Your Life*, appeared on the bookstore shelves. It has a good chapter on grief dreams as well as chapters on losses in situations other than death. Another recent book, *Breakthrough Dreaming* by Gayle Delaney, discusses mourning dreams. Both of these authors are psychologists; however, their books are quite readable by non-specialists.

While I was living in Switzerland for a brief time, I found at the Jung Institute a marvelous book written by a professor of psychology at the University of Zurich. Entitled *A Time to Mourn*, this book features dreams as valuable guidance in the task of mourning. The author, Verena Kast, uses an individual's dream series and other dreams to illustrate this.

Mary Jane Moffat's anthology, *In the Midst of Winter: Selections from the Literature of Mourning*, is a unique book about the process and nature of grief, which developed out of her own grief for her husband. It includes the place of dreams in the grieving process and shares selections from authors who have experienced grief.

Grieving: How to Go on Living When Someone You Love Dies, by Therese Rando, is another good resource book to which I will frequently refer. I find it helpful to think of the grieving process as "tasks," as Rando's book presents it (225). I list them here in order to use them as references in discussing specific dreams. The tasks of grieving may occur all at once in a dream, but usually one aspect will be predominate in both waking and dreaming states of grieving:

- acknowledging and understanding the loss
- experiencing the pain and reacting to the separation
- moving adaptively into the new life without forgetting the old.

Acknowledgments

I wish to thank all those who so generously shared their dreams and bereavement experiences, so many I dare not attempt to name them; others for their interest and encouragement; and my husband, Bill, for his practical assistance such as picking up books from the library and taking me out to eat on busy days. I especially want to express deepest gratitude to Ashli Peake, who turned the first raw draft into a first manuscript with her computer—without her, there would be no book. I also extend thanks to those copyright holders who granted permission to reprint the following copyrighted material:

From *The Variety of Dream Experiences*, © 1987 Nan Zimmerman. Used with permission.

From *Something More* by Catherine Marshall, © 1974 Chosen Books, Inc., a division of Baker Book House Company, Grand Rapids, Michigan.

From *A Time to Mourn* by Verena Kast, © 1988 Daimon Verlag, Einsiedeln, Switzerland.

Reprinted from *Pastoral Care and Counseling in Grief* by Wayne E. Oates, copyright © 1976 Fortress Press. Used by permission of Augsburg Fortress.

From *Peace, Love and Healing* by Bernie S. Siegel, MD. Copyright © 1989 by Bernard S. Siegel, MD. Published by HarperCollins.

Acknowledgments

From *The Dream Game* by Ann Faraday. Copyright © 1974 by AFAR Publishers A.G. Published by HarperCollins.

Extracts from "Infidelity" by Olga Berggolts, translation © 1974 Daniel Weissbort, published in *Post-War Russian Poetry* ©1974 Penguin Books.

Reprinted with permission from Therese A. Rando, *Grieving: How to Go on Living When Someone You Love Dies*. Copyright © 1988 by Jossey-Bass Inc., Publishing. First published by Lexington Books. All rights reserved.

From *The Meaning in Dreams and Dreaming* by Maria F. Mahoney © 1966 Citadel Press.

From *Dreams and Spiritual Growth* by Louis Savory © 1984 Paulist Press.

From *Dreams in the Psychology of Religion* by James Gollnick ©1987 The Edwin Mellen Press/Lewiston, New York.

From *In the Midst of Winter*, edited by Mary Jane Moffat, © 1982 Random House, Inc.

From *A Book of Angels* by Sophy Burnham. Copyright © 1990 by Sophy Burnham. Reprinted by permission of Ballantine Books, a Division of Random House, Inc.

From "Sisters Are Like Shadows of Our Other Selves" by Rheta Grimsley Johnson, copyright 1991 The Commercial Appeal, Memphis, Tennessee. Used with permission.

From *On Dreams and Death* by Marie-Louise von Franz, © 1984. Reprinted by arrangement with Shambhala Publications, Inc., 300 Massachusetts Avenue, Boston, Massachusetts 02115.

From *The Biographical Memoirs of St. John Bosco* by Giovanni Battista Lemoyne, SDB, et al., translated by Diego Borgatello, SDB. © 1964- Salesiana Publishers.

From *Dreams: God's Forgotten Language* by John Sanford, © 1968 HarperCollins.

From *The Dream Below the Sun* © 1981. Translated by Willis Barnstone. Published by The Crossing Press: Freedom, California.

The Scripture quotations contained herein are from the New Revised Standard Version of the Bible, copyrighted, 1989 by the Division of Christian Education of the National Council of the Churches of Christ in the United States of America, and are used by permission. All rights reserved.

Introduction

Dreams in which a deceased loved one appears have been shared with me since the publication of my book on the place of dreams in the Bible, *Discovering My Biblical Dream Heritage*. Bereaved persons who have shared such dreams usually have done so with reservations because they did not know such dreams are a normal part of grieving. Nor did they know how their dreams would be received. Mourning dreams are of such a personal nature that the dreamer normally hesitates to reveal them.

All dreams are personal, and those in which the deceased appear are especially personal. Frequently the dreamer is fearful that by sharing the dream some of its special quality might be diminished or diluted. The dreamer is not sure the one listening to it will understand. Others might think that it is strange to make anything of "just a dream." If it is a pleasant dream, it might be discounted as "wishful thinking" and not as facing reality.

I have found little written about dreams of the bereaved. What is available is usually written for those in the counseling profession. Altogether, though, I have found a recognition that dreams reflect the mourning process.[1] But most mourners do not know

---

1 See articles by Moody and Gerne. Gerne's report on her study of mourning and dreams is another example of this recognition. The study was undertaken at the Psychological Institute of the University of Zurich, Switzerland. It covers the dreams of a woman over the period of time between 1937 and

that this is normal. Actually, more recognition of dreams as part of the mourning process is mentioned in literature written by the bereaved as part of their grieving process.

In this book I wish to show the value of dreams in the process of starting life without the deceased loved one or after any kind of loss. This is a book for those who mourn.

The dreams shared here can show us how they provide an inner resource for resolving grief. Keep in mind that, while there are some elements that are common to these dreams of the bereaved, the content will be as individual as the individuals who dream them.

When I started out, I organized the dreams according to the phases of mourning which are generally familiar to most people. The results were not what I wanted. Dreams, like grief, do not fit neatly into phases. While using phases or stages has meaning for the counselor, I found it not so helpful for those in mourning. They are not experiencing feelings and the altered circumstances of life in a neat, forward-moving outline with a conclusion; rather they are experiencing more of a process that goes in circles. The British author C. S. Lewis wrote this following his wife's death: "One keeps emerging from a phase, but it always recurs. Round and round. Everything repeats. Am I going in circles?" (67). As

---

1985 and deals with the deaths of four members of her family. The aim of Gerne's study was to evaluate the mourning process indications in dream content as an example of problem-solving. My own particular interest in this study is that it demonstrates that dreams do reflect the mourning process.

Situations in which the deceased were dead or dying in her dreams occurred after each death. Dreams of the deceased were most frequent immediately after the death events. Dreams became less frequent in the fifth to seventh month of mourning and continued to decrease. The most frequent emotion experienced in her dreams after each death was apprehension. Both apprehension and sadness increased after each death but were significantly more frequent after the death of a husband. Three phases of the mourning process were recognizable in the dreams. The first phase consisted of dreams concerned with death, the deceased, and sadness. The second phase could be identified with the appearance of themes such as work, new orientations, and living characters. Finally, there was fading out of these concerns in the dream content by the middle of the year. Of course, there was an overlapping of dream content among the phases.

we look at these dreams and all dreams, remember that dreams tend to exaggerate to get our attention.

Identifying grief dreams by the four categories of dreams used by Loma Flowers, a psychiatrist, is useful to me in describing the kinds of insights they offer. She uses them in general dream work; I do not know that she uses them with grief dreams at all. These are described by Gayle Delaney in *Breakthrough Dreaming* (225), who adds two other categories of dreams, integration and problem-solving dreams. I will list all six of them here and use April's dreams after her husband's death to illustrate them.

1. Dreams That Bring to Attention New Information
   Not Yet Assimilated (Emphasis Dreams)

2. Dreams That Bring the Dreamer Face-to-Face
   with Realities That Have Not Been Accepted
   (Confronting Dreams)

3. Dreams That Present Useful and Meaningful
   Information for Dealing with What the Dreamer
   Already Knows (Reconceptualization Dreams)

4. Dreams That Help the Dreamer Discover
   New Information about Herself or Himself
   or about Some Aspect of Self (Discovery Dreams)

5. Dreams That Report to the Dreamer
   the Progress Being Made on the Use
   of a Recently Gained Insight (Integration Dreams)

6. Dreams That Help Solve Problems
   (Problem-Solving Dreams)

Dreams That Bring to Attention New Information Not Yet Assimilated (Emphasis Dreams)

April's first dream underlines the fact that her husband's death had actually happened. (For a discussion of this dream and her other dreams in this category, see chapter 2.)

> I saw my husband, Orie, in a dream. He was wearing his
> Gideon emblem pin on his lapel, and it was glowing like
> a light. He was sitting with a group of people. He turned
> and smiled a dazzling smile at me and said, "I'm sorry I
> had to let you think I was dead." I felt so many mixed
> feelings. I was happy to see him, and yet I was almost
> angry because he didn't seem upset about leaving me at
> all. I wanted to stay with him, but the phone rang and
> woke me up.

April's husband died suddenly and unexpectedly. This dream
reflects that she had difficulty taking in what had happened,
which is natural. The shock of beginning grief has been described
as "an amazement that what was alive and of this world only a
few moments ago is irrevocably gone" (Moffat 3). Also, the
dream's portrayal of Orie wearing the suit he was buried in and
his behavior toward her underlines the fact that he was no longer
with her.

Dreams That Bring the Dreamer Face-to-Face
with Realities That Have Not Been Accepted
(Confronting Dreams)

This may seem to be the same as the emphasis dreams just
discussed; in a way most grief dreams are confronting, for they
reinforce what has happened. However, this kind goes further
and confronts the dreamer with what is to be done about it.

In April's second dream she is confronted not only with Orie's
death but with the changes that this brings to her life. Now she
has to look out for herself, and this is frightening, so frightening
that she thinks it evil and invokes the name of Jesus.

> I was looking under the bed, checking as I always did in
> closets and in the house when I came back in from being
> out. I was on my knees looking under the bed, and
> when I straightened up, arms went around my waist from
> behind. I looked down at the arms and thought, Oh,
> good, it's Orie. Then I looked over my shoulder and

there was Orie's face. For just a second I was so happy.
Then a voice that seemed to come from inside me said,
"No, no! It's not Orie! It just looks like him." This terrible
fear started at the top of my head and went to my feet.
I've never been so frightened in my life. I remembered
what I had been taught and said, "In the name of Jesus,
get out!"

In this searching behavior I see April hoping to find her
husband and wishing that he were there and that things were as
they were before. This searching-finding-separating routine gives
the mourner practice in accepting the loss. At the same time it
underscores what the dreamer knows—that the dead is really
dead (Kast 59-63).[2] In addition to this emphasis, April is confronted with what she must do now to take care of herself.
Checking her house for safety purposes is the dream's way of
saying she must do everything for herself now.

Dreams That Present Useful
and Meaningful Information
for Dealing with What the Dreamer Already Knows
(Reconceptualization Dreams)

It was some time before April had another dream. This dream
did not have April's husband in it, but she connected it to previous
ones about him.

I dreamed the door blew open. This frightened me. Then
I saw there was a storm with both dust and hail in it. I
thought, That doesn't mix. As I awakened I thought of
my children. Were they okay?

---

2 Kast's book contains an excellent discussion of the searching behavior of
the grief-stricken. She describes searching as "as attempt to preserve old
familiar ways," as "resistance against change." Besides the actual searching
for the deceased in physical places, the search may take place in other forms
such as inner dialogue with the deceased and the telling of stories about
the deceased person. The search is an involuntary behavior; it is important
not to urge the mourner to give up what may seem like aimless searching.

April had this dream when she was staying in my home along with my sister and others. She was mixing social pleasantries with grieving. Was this like mixing dust and hail on some level of consciousness? Was this dream, resulting in concern for her children, presenting her with the need to be concerned with the living and thus with her own life?

Dreams That Help the Dreamer
Discover New Information about Herself or Himself
or about Some Aspect of Self (Discovery Dreams)

This information may not be new so much as it has been denied or repressed by the dreamer. In her fourth dream April discovers she is able not only to look after herself but others. This was something she had not felt able to do previously. She also discovers that a new relationship with her husband is possible and that pleasant memories of him did not trouble her so much.

> I was in a motel room with some children (I think they were grandchildren) and my daughter, Joy. I went into the hall across from us and found two blonde-haired women who had been killed. I ran back into our room trying to hide what had happened from the children, as they wanted to go out. I told Joy what happened and we had hamburgers brought in for the children. I looked out the door and there was Orie and a policeman putting a cover over the dead girls. I felt so much love in my heart and thought, That's just like Orie, taking care of everything for me. I felt his protection again and it felt so good. In my dream he came and sat down at the table with me. I saw that lock of hair that always fell down on his forehead, and I reached over and brushed it back. I felt very happy—like old times. I woke up right after that. I felt more at peace after this dream.

Dreams That Report to the Dreamer the Progress Being Made on the Use of a Recently Gained Insight (Integration Dreams)

The fourth dream just discussed with discovery dreams also reports to April that she has taken on some of Orie's skills and qualities, such as the ability to protect and care for herself and others. This feels good, just as if Orie were still alive and looking after her.

Dreams That Help Solve Problems (Problem-Solving Dreams)

Grief dreams are a resource to the dreamer for solving the problem of learning to live without the physical presence of the absent loved one. To some degree, we observe this in April's dreams; however, problem-solving is a more dominant theme in other dreams than in hers.

If you look back to the tasks of grieving presented by Therese Rando in the Preface, you will see how these categories of dreams correspond with and help April accomplish these tasks. The first dream helps her acknowledge her loss and make what has happened real. The second dream helps her experience the pain of separation. The third and fourth dreams nudge her into moving adaptively into her new life without forgetting the old.

In this book, instead of grouping dreams according to categories or elements of grief found in them, I have grouped them according to the dreamers. This keeps them connected to the persons who dreamed them. This arrangement seems less likely to tempt me to fit them into a pattern that might distort their meaning. I found that most of us are deeply touched by another's dream and relate to the person rather than to a category. My main purpose is to help you know that dreams during bereavement are normal and healing.

PART 1

Dreams Shared with Me

Even when the dead have ebbed in memory from our waking hours, they may return to us in dreams. These reunions, often startlingly vivid in their imagery, are sometimes comforting. Or, on wakening, they may leave us feeling bereft, as if our unconscious is reminding us that we have not yet fully accepted the cruelty of the loss or have feelings still to be resolved. — Mary Jane Moffat, Introduction to "Dreaming the Dead," *In the Midst of Winter*

These dreams of the bereaved were shared with me in response to my interest in dreams. I think of them as special offerings to all humankind. The courageous sharing of these personal dreams can help us when people in our lives die. The dreams are mysterious, haunting, scary, beautiful, sad, and joyful, as all dreams are, and they are much more.

Usually dreamers like to have their names used. Where I have used the dreamer's name, I have first received permission. When I was unable to get in touch with the dreamer, I modified the names and circumstances.

Many dreams shared with me are not included; they would take another book. Yet all the dreams made their way into this book in that they contributed to my understanding of the dreams of the bereaved and of how dreams benefit the grieving dreamer.

As you read these dreams, think of the courage that sharing them may have taken. The dreamers not only had to delve into their grief but then had to face the prevailing social attitude about dreams that equates dreaming with imagination. Dreaming and imagination are not valued as "reality" in Western culture. In some cultures it is not necessary to value one above the other. The sharing of our dreams may be a small step toward valuing inner reality as well as outer reality.

1. Dreams about Deceased Parents and Grandparents

Dreams help us mourn our dead parents. They may show us their suffering, reminding us how it was for them and for us. Dreams may give us happy memories. They may help us cry. They may present our parent giving comfort. They may help us deal with issues resulting from the changes that death has brought.

Crying in Dreams

Allen, a young lawyer, experienced several deaths, all in less than a year. Besides the deaths in his family, he mourned the death of an older lawyer who had been his mentor. Dreaming accompanied these death events and helped Allen cry.

Allen's father lived alone and had been dead several days before his body was discovered. This is the dream Allen had several weeks later, as told to me on June 20, 1990:

> I am at my father's funeral. It is being held in the hog
> house on my father's farm. The person directing it is the
> tenant farmer. A film is being shown. My father appears
> with two brown-and-white puppies. He is enjoying them.
> I woke up crying.

After an aunt's death, Allen dreamed she was on a sofa and he was beside her. They had talked pleasantly and now they were saying goodbye and comforting each other. He woke up in tears again. His aunt had died on the anniversary of his mother's death, and the pain of losing her may have surfaced again.

Both dreams helped Allen release and express his sadness and reinforce the reality of the deaths on an emotional level. The setting for his father's funeral is reminiscent of the biblical story of Lazarus' death. Lazarus had been dead four days by the time Jesus arrived at his village and asked the sisters Mary and Martha to take away the stone of his tomb. Martha's response was, "But, Lord, by this time there is a bad odor." Allen was perplexed about why the funeral was held in the hog house. I gently asked him if the hog house reminded him of anything in his waking life, but nothing came to mind. Perhaps questions like "What does a hog house smell like?" and "What did your father's house smell like at the time his body was discovered?" would have helped him make the connection. He had already told me that the house had to be fumigated and the carpets removed; however, I felt he was still too close to the experience to explore it further at that time.

To attend to the last part of the dream was more comforting for him, and that is what he seemed to need at the moment. The film shown in the dream depicted memories of his father and two of his favorite dogs. The dogs had died sometime earlier and now his father was with them. The dream was saying, "Although your father's death has been a tragic experience for you, it hasn't been so bad for your father. He has what he needs for his happiness. Think back on more pleasant memories as the film suggests."

The Event As It Was Recalled

My friend, Barbara, had a curious dream about a month after her mother's death:

Mother was spitting on people. I think we were in an
eating place in a shopping mall. Then Mother became
lost in the shopping mall and I searched for her.

Barbara's mother had Alzheimer's disease. This is probably
one of the most devastating and frustrating illnesses that can
affect a family because of the way it confuses the patient's mind
and affects behavior. Watching her mother become more and
more irrational, even accusing Barbara and others unjustly and
sometimes kicking at them, left Barbara with unpleasant memories to disengage from after the death. This dream recalled what
it was like in the last weeks before Barbara's mother died. Until
the end, Barbara had taken her mother and a few friends out to
lunch on Sundays. Although her mother had never spit on
anyone, she had been difficult to handle. The dream seems to
have exaggerated the behavior, depicting Barbara's fear that even
worse behavior might occur. Furthermore, exaggeration is a
characteristic of dreams.

Patients with Alzheimer's wander away; they become confused and get lost if they are not watched. Searching for her
mother or the fear of having to search for her may have been
part of Barbara's waking experience, which the dream was
reviewing. Also, the loss through death seemed as if her mother
had just wandered away. Searching is often part of both waking
and dreaming experience and is mentioned in accounts of
grieving. Sometimes it takes the form of expecting to find the
deceased person in the usual place doing the usual things.

We may wonder why dreams sometimes take us back over
the unpleasant days just before death occurs. These disturbing
dreams come early in the grieving process. They bring into
awareness information that is not quite new but still has not
become familiar. Dreams seek to help us bring our lives into
harmony with what has happened and to put words with the
experience. Dreams that occur even years later when the grief
has been resolved are usually pleasant and confirm that the
dreamer has worked out the grief. Barbara has not yet had such
a dream, and she may not. This does not mean that she is not
resolving her grief, simply that she has not recalled such a dream.

Many people do not recall grief dreams, some recall dreams in early grief, some in later grief, and some throughout the grieving process.

The Disturbing Appearance
of the Deceased Ill and Dying

Donna and her husband had moved back to their home state of Kansas, so she was with her family for some time before their deaths. This may account for the way her father and stepmother appeared in her dreams; they were as sick as they had been before their deaths. Also, this may have been the dreams' way of identifying them as her father and stepmother. I think the message conveyed by the dreams was, "It's finally over."

Donna's father died of a heart attack. Afterward Donna felt as though a cloud were following her around. Then she had a disturbing and startling dream in which her father appeared lying in the casket:

> It was not just that he was in the casket. It was the way
> he looked and what he did. He appeared the way he
> looked before he died, thin with a drawn expression and
> not smiling, as if this weren't disturbing enough he raised
> up and lay back down. He did this several times looking
> miserable all the while. Finally, he was able to say,
> "Okay," and lay down and stayed down. After this dream
> the feeling of the cloud following me left.

Donna's stepmother died of lung cancer and a bad heart. For the last two days of her life, she had been on a ventilator and unable to talk. Donna had this dream several weeks after her stepmother's death:

> She appeared as she was at death with a badly curved
> back and very sick. I called her by name and said, "I
> thought you were gone from us." Then I awakened and
> realized that she really was dead.

In my own dreams, and in most dreams that have been shared with me, the deceased have appeared healthy and happy and in the prime of life; so I find these dreams in which the deceased appear sick unusual. Nevertheless, the dreams helped Donna become used to the information by conveying the message, "It's finally over." Her startling dreams were helping her assimilate the reality of her father's and stepmother's deaths.

This is what grief is. C. M. Parkes in "The First Year of Bereavement" defines grief as a process of realization, of "making real" the fact of loss (465).[1] Until loss becomes real, we cannot make the adjustment needed to live without the loved one. Dreams can help make this loss real.

San Francisco psychologist Alan Siegel writes about dreams in which his grandfather appeared sick and gaunt. He had died from stomach cancer after a long, lingering illness. This series of dreams ended before Alan had a chance to talk with his grandfather. Although these dreams were painful, reflecting on them helped Siegel work through his grief.

Unlike Donna, he also had dreams that focused on pleasant memories. In one dream his grandfather appeared restored to health in a beautiful setting. He was in an orange grove, where ripe oranges hung from the trees and the grass and leaves were very green. Siegel walked with his grandfather, and as they walked, his grandfather gave him advice about his career and encouraged him to stay in school. This dream helped Alan realize that he had reached a resolution to his grieving (4-5).

Perhaps Donna did not need this additional touch in dreams to help her feel she was resolving her grief, or perhaps such comfort would come later.

---

1 This is a study of the reaction of London widows to the death of their husbands. "It [grief] is a process of realization, of making psychologically real an external event which is not desired and for which coping plans do not exist."

Life Without the Loved One

One week before the sixth-month anniversary of Mother's death, I had a dream. I am at my parents' home in Georgia and in their bedroom. I am snuggled up with blankets and pillows in their bed. I am looking at old family pictures. I look up at the wall and think, "Daddy is changing the pictures on the wall." I don't know if he is taking pictures down or putting new pictures up. It is like he is in process. I wonder if the pictures on the wall are a good idea. I hear Mother call me as she is coming from downstairs, "Jane?" as if she is wondering where I am and what I am doing. She sees me in their bedroom and comes in. She first throws a pillow at the foot of the bed as if she is going to lay down with me and look at the pictures with me. This is something I used to enjoy doing with her.

Friskie, my mother's cat, is in the room going crazy playing and crawling up under the top layer of covers like cats will do.

I look up to see Mother standing across the room. She looks so beautiful. I know when I see her that she is Spirit yet very real and present with me. Her hair is beautiful like she likes it. She is dressed in an off-white to beige gown with sparkles in it like an evening gown. The gown is long-sleeved with no sewn seams. The gown covers her feet and sort of disappears into the floor, spirit-like.

I look down to the picture that I am holding in my hand. It is a rather large black and white picture of Mother's baptism at age seventeen. She is very young and pretty. The picture is like some of the pictures of my mother I have seen of her when she is young, but I have never seen a picture of her baptism. She is dressed in a white dress. As I look at the picture, the picture takes action. I see Mother very happy walking down a crowded hill to a river to be baptized. Before she reaches the river a man picks her up over his head and another

man throws a bucket of water on her. She screams in
surprise. I wake up, puzzled about this rude awakening.
The dream is so real and beautiful to end in such a crude
way (Hendricks 180).

Jane was a student who was living away from home at the
time of her mother's death. She had to return to classes, so she
did not have to face the change in daily routine brought about
by the loss of her mother. Nevertheless, life was changing, as her
dream shows her by her father's changing the pictures on the
wall. These new pictures now imply pictures without her mother.
"In process" implies her father is moving through his grief. She
is not sure she is ready to look at the new pictures.

Jane's dream took her through pleasant memories (the way
looking at pictures does) with her mother. It showed her the
things she would miss—feeling the warmth and coziness of her
parents' bedroom, looking at pictures together, playing with the
cat. Then her dream pictured her mother's being baptized to a
new life that was different from her physical life with its
limitations. Seeing her mother looking beautiful in death helped
Jane acknowledge her loss on a deeper level. Finally, experiencing the pain of her own life being forever changed was a shock,
as much of a shock as seeing her mother dashed with a bucket
of water.

Put another way, Jane's dream states (pictures) life as changing
because her mother is being baptized. (In the Bible baptism by
immersion into water—a symbol of cleansing—depicts death,
burial, and resurrection to a new life. This is what it means in
Jane's experience.) Therefore, everything that her mother stood
for in her life—comfort, support, enjoyment—was gone. Realizing this loss was like being dashed with a bucket of water.

This surprising conclusion to her dream awakened Jane to the
fact of life without her mother. But this did not happen until she
had been comforted with memories through pictures and had
been given a beautiful new picture of her mother to remember
and enrich her ongoing life.

The Spiritual Quality of Light

Karen was only twenty-seven when her father died after a two-year battle with cancer. She was very grieved. One night, after she had cried herself to sleep, she had a dream that was so clear that she felt she was actually awake. Unlike her other dreams that usually faded from memory, she has remembered this dream for many years:

> My father appeared to me in a nebulous light by my bed.
> He told me he was all right and spoke something
> comforting, which I couldn't remember when I woke up. As
> he departed down the hall, he took on a spiritual quality.
> He was more than my father. He was, also, Abba/Father.

"Abba" is a biblical word associated with God. Karen saw her father as more than just her earthly father. Light is an especially beautiful symbol. It comes from God and symbolizes life and awareness. Karen's father appears in light with a heavenly message. We say that someone who grasps an idea or begins to understand something better is "seeing the light." Could the dream have helped Karen see her father's death in a new light? As Karen recalled her dream, it was apparent that she had been helped to grasp the reality of her father's death. She was comforted to know that he was all right even though he must live life in another form in order to be all right.

Mysterious Dreams and Dream-like Experiences

Katie is my cousin. Her mother was my Aunt Neva. About a year after Aunt Neva's death, I was visiting my family in Oklahoma and Katie shared three dreams with me. Her mother does not appear in these dreams as herself, but there is no doubt that they are related to her mother's death in Katie's mind. Departed loved ones do not always appear in the dreams of the bereaved.

I am providing the following brief background of both Katie and her dream to help you understand the unbelievable suffering involved. Such a difficult experience may account for the content of the dream.

For fourteen months Katie had stayed with her dying mother. Through her pain and physical weakness, Aunt Neva had comforted Katie as Katie had cared for her. She had had almost no functioning heart left and at her own request had been allowed to go home to die.

During this time Aunt Neva lived almost as if she were in a dream. There was no difference between the past, present, or future; they were all one. Yet she was aware of those living around her and what was happening. To Aunt Neva, her departed husband and grandchildren were with her as much as those who were still living. She cried for her own Papa whom she saw hurting, although he had been dead for over sixty years. She wanted to "go home," but she did not want to leave her children.

Once, when Katie groaned with a back pain, Aunt Neva tried to crawl over the bed rail and come to Katie's aid, saying, "Something's the matter with my Katie." She was also in touch with angels; she told Katie the angel said it was all right for her to lie down beside her.[2] When Katie groaned in pain, Aunt Neva put a little white satin pillow across her back, and then put both arms around Katie, patting her and hugging her.

Katie calls these nurturing and comforting gestures "a gift of incredible beauty." Her own daughter, Nita, who was staying the

---

2 As you read this, you may think it rather strange that Aunt Neva was not surprised that an angel spoke to her. Even John Woolman (a Quaker mystic who lived in the 1700s), when hearing the song of the holy angel in a near-death state, called it a mystery and an "uncommon circumstance" (Kepler 219-21).

You would have to know Aunt Neva to know that an angel speaking to her would not seem unusual. Also, it would be natural for her to speak of the angel, as she did here, as if the angel were an ordinary presence like the nurse. She had a simple uncomplicated faith in God that remained strong through the many difficulties of life. Aunt Neva always saw things through the eyes of love; she saw through and beyond imperfections, faults, and failures. This was because she let God's love flow through her to and from others. In her last days she acknowledged this need of love from others when she said to her Home Health Nurse, "I needed you, I need gentle." No wonder Aunt Neva did not think it unusual for an angel to speak to her, she was an angel herself.

night, awoke and looked over to the bed in which they were sleeping in this manner. To her astonishment she saw them bathed in light. The light was not from far back in the kitchen nor was it from the tiny night-light in the almost-closed bathroom. Both Katie and Nita were convinced an angel was there with them.

A week after her mother's death, Katie had this first dream experience accompanied by sleepwalking. This is an emphasis dream in which what has happened is made more real:

> I awoke sometime in the middle of the night. I was stumbling around in the room and got up in the middle of the other bed where all her [mother's] clothes were stacked. I was in a panic because she was gone. In some dream place, I heard her moving about and thought she needed me. I heard her calling me, and it was much too real. Then I really awoke and knew it was okay to go back to bed. It wasn't really sad, but I don't want to do it again.

Katie said she could understand having such a dream, because she had been hypervigilant for so long and, even in her sleep, she had been tuned into her mother's slightest move. What had really startled Katie was finding herself in the middle of her mother's bed. She had never walked in her sleep before.

"This next dream is the first of several filled with numbers, lots of color, black, hideous shades of purple and green that made me nauseous," Katie wrote. She wished that if there were to be comforting dreams, they would arrive quickly.

> I was with three little old women. They were all dressed in black with black scarves over their heads. They went with me into an elevator of a building I used to work in. I kept trying to go to the fifteenth floor although I knew that building had only seven floors. Finally, I got them out on the eighth floor and was so proud that I had rescued them. They were lost and I hunted frantically and finally saw them in the elevator again and went with them to the ground floor. We started up a street that was totally bare of people and in the distance saw a tree.

There was a huge swarm of bees in it so I told them to
wait. I watched them go down three steps to a landing,
up three steps to street level, back down the three steps,
over and over again. I started to the tree but looked by
the side of the street and a huge thing was growing out
of it and it was alive. I thought, oh, My Dear God, that is
totally evil. I hurried on by but the swarm of bees was all
around me. I looked back and the three little women
were still going up and down the steps, and I thought,
Well, they will be okay until someone comes for them. I
was just standing, waiting while the bees swarmed
around me, when I awoke.

Katie sees the three women as representing her mother and
two aunts, her mother's sisters. Her taking care of them in this
dream reflects her feeling of being responsible for so long a time
for her mother. She seems to feel some responsibility for her
aunts as well. The bees signify pain, sharp and stinging. The evil
thing must mean death. So we see that Katie has already
associated this dream with the death of her mother. She recognized the intense feeling she experienced preceding the death
as well as when the death occurred.

This is Katie's dream and only she can say what her dream
means to her.[3] At the time she experienced it as a nauseating
nightmare and did not indicate that she wanted to explore the
images. Dream specialists tend to believe that when you listen
to a dream, you "should respect the dreamer's desire not to go
deeper into certain images" (Bosnak 35). However, to show you
the possibilities, I want to examine these images. Remember that
these are my interpretations and may not be correct for the
dreamer.

- **An office building with an elevator.** This is the
  opening setting. It reminds Katie of the building in
  which she used to work because it has seven
  floors. No one else is in the building.

---

3 "Ultimately, it is only the dreamer who can correctly interpret a dream, not
an outside source, be it a book, friend, or analyst" (Guiley xiii).

- **The dreamer and three little old women dressed in black.** The whole image is the dreamer with three little old women wearing black. They go together to make one image that represents a person in grief. We know she/they are in grief because the little old women wear black, the color of mourning. By using three women instead of one, the dream emphasizes how engulfing her grief and the whole lengthy experience of her mother's dying are. This is the dream's way of underlining the dreamer in grief. The language of dreams is mostly in pictures; so it seems reasonable that dreams underscore the importance or size of something by repeating images.[4]

- **Major action in the first part of the dream.** The dreamer and the women (grief with its feelings of anger, confusion, and sadness) are in the elevator and are searching for a safe place to get off. Finally they get off on the ground floor (they are back where they started). In other words, the dreamer is going about the business of grieving in her life (building). Her grief (an elevator in the building) takes her on ups and downs as she searches. Katie's next action is to walk along an empty street. In other words, she leaves grief and starts to pursue further meaning for her life in this experience.

- **A living tree with a huge, evil-looking growth.** This tree depicts life, perhaps the dreamer's life,

---

4 In the Bible, emphasis is conventionally expressed by using threes, as "This is the temple of the LORD, the temple of the LORD, the temple of the LORD" (Jer 7:4); "Holy, holy, holy" (Isa 6:3); and the triple blessing (Num 6:24-26). Emphasis is made in poetry this way, too, as in these lines by May Sarton: "Did some say that there would be an end, an end, Oh, an end to love and mourning?"

and something more that the dreamer interprets as evil. Dreams sometimes exaggerate, so this evil thing may not be so evil. Still it has grown out of the living of her life and it is distressing.

- **The three women repeatedly go up and down three stairs.** The number three may have some significance, but I see the whole image as meaning that grief can become habitual. This may be the evil thing that Katie sees when she observes the growth on the tree.

- **A swarm of bees.** The bees swarm around Katie, but they do not sting. The scripture, "O death, where is thy sting?" (1 Cor 15:55) comes to mind, but there is a very personal meaning and message in the image of the swarming bees. Bees are by nature orderly. When they swarm, they are actually reorganizing their social structure. Are the bees saying that a way out of this habitual mourning is to reach out and begin anew, building on the insights gained from what has gone before?

Katie had another dream in which she and a beautiful young woman whom she thought of as her mother cross back and forth across the border of another country (perhaps life after life on earth?). They pretend to be actors and dancers to escape getting caught (in suffering?). Katie feels she is not appropriately dressed, and they go to her sister Nancy's to look for a change of clothes. They have to go up seventeen steps, which are covered with a slick lime green bedspread. Here she loses her mother and searches for her. Katie wants to go to her mother's house where her clothes are. A strange man (Katie thinks he represents her father) wants her mother to get into a boat and go with him, because he loves her. She wants to go, but walks away saying, "But what about my babies, what about my babies?" Katie said, "To me, this dream was Mother wanting to go where Daddy was and yet not wanting to leave us kids, as she said over and over before she died."

The dream is also about Katie and her experience with her dying mother who had so much difficulty letting go of her earthly loved ones. Climbing a flight of stairs covered with a slick, lime green bedspread brings to mind the almost impossible, nauseating task of caring for her mother through her long period of suffering. Yet, having lost her mother to death, Katie still searches for her because she cannot get used to not having her around.[5] These dreams confront Katie with the reality of her mother's death and help her get used to it.

With all its steps, Katie's dream reminds me of a poem written by Linda Pastan after she had been told the five stages of grief. She compares going through the stages to climbing stairs following an amputation. After climbing denial, anger, and bargaining, she slid downstairs with depression. Then she climbed out on hope until she saw what she was climbing toward—acceptance. She struggled on, reaching acceptance only to discover that grief is a circular staircase, for, as she says, "I have lost you."

About two years later Katie finally had her comforting experience. She could not say that it was a dream. Actually it sounds more like a near-death experience.

---

5 See Viorst (262-63) for a discussion of the death of parents who have lived full and fulfilling lives. She says we are never ready to give up our mothers and fathers. Once she told a friend whose mother had died at age eighty-nine, "Well, she certainly had a chance to live a full life." Her friend responded angrily, "I hate it when people say that she lived a full life, as if I therefore shouldn't feel sad that she's dead. I'm going to miss her."

My father was eighty-two when he died. I was ready for his suffering to end. Seven years later I still miss him.

The timing of death is never right. There is never an ideal time for any kind of separation. Sometimes death is too late; for example, when a person lives on in an irreversible coma or with life support and no possibility of recovery.

When a child's parent dies, it is too early, and that child may search into adult life for the parent. My grandmother died when my mother was less than two years old. She was cared for by loving grandparents, but when her mother's letters—those she had written and those that had been written to her—were discovered not too long ago, it was like finding her mother. The letters began with the first child and went through the birth of the third, my mother.

After surgery, while she was in intensive care for several days with heart problems, pneumonia, extremely low blood pressure, and a low platelet count, Katie was given the wrong medicine by mistake. Her blood pressure started to drop and she had the following experience. It is not an ordinary dream. Perhaps it should not be called a dream; but it is an altered state of consciousness, and it is a part of her bereavement experience. This is what she wrote in a letter to her Aunt Carrie:

> I looked down at all these people who were around my bed and thought, This is dying, and this isn't bad at all. I don't have any pain. I remember being amazed at what was going on. Then I looked around and there was Daddy sitting in a chair. One hand was up at the side of his face, just like he sat so much of the time, and there was a twinkle in his eyes, but he said nothing, just looked at me. Then I saw Mother, her face had that soft glow she always had when she was happy about something. She took a step to me and laid her hand against the side of my face in that gentle way she had of touching. I was instantly back in my body on the bed. When I opened my eyes, I wanted to touch the side of my face as it felt warm where she had touched me.

In discussion Katie said the following:

> I can't say what actually happened to me. Yet my perception of it was and is that I had been with my parents, and they had sent me back, that it was not my time to leave this world. ...I firmly believe I was allowed that brief encounter with my parents, [to know] that they are together and happy, and that I will one day be allowed to see them again. I no longer fear death, no longer fear the process of dying.

A Change in Daily Routine Occurs

Lilian Lim of Singapore was thirty-two when her father died from abdominal cancer after spending the last three months of his life at home. Here is her dream introduced with some background explanation:

> My father's room was opposite mine. Our doors faced each other. My father woke early and usually had the six o'clock news on his radio very softly. On days when the doors were ajar, I could hear the radio softly.
>
> I dreamed I was waking one morning. I woke up in my dream and turned my head to see the door. It was ajar, but I wondered why I couldn't hear the radio. Then I remembered my father had died.

Everything throughout the day, from waking up to going to sleep, seems to be associated with the absent loved one. By calling attention to the change in daily events, Lilian's dream helped her grasp the reality of her father's death.

Cremation and Interment

Mary DeLaine is the daughter of my university houseparents. They died within a few months of each other after lengthy illnesses. She is grateful that she had the opportunity of caring for them when they needed her. She writes the following in a letter about her dreams following her father's death and cremation. (Mary DeLaine had brought her parents to Hope, Arkansas, where she lived, to care for them, but they wanted to be buried with family in another state. This entered into the decision for cremation.)

> Through the years I have been one of those persons who claims not to dream while sleeping. Once in a while, upon waking, I may have a fleeting recollection of a dream. After I married, I was almost jealous of my husband because he seemed to dream several episodes each night and could recount them to me in detail. When I have remembered a dream, it was usually a "bad dream."
>
> Several years before my parents died, they had made plans and requested to be cremated at the time of their

death. When the hospital called about my mother's passing, Daddy said to me, "I'm not sure about carrying out our plans." After evaluating the situation, we went the more traditional route because of Daddy's desires.

I do not recall any dreams relating to the time during my mother's illness nor to her death and thereafter.

When Daddy died, it was my responsibility to make the decision as to whether to carry out his previous plan or not. Again, because of the circumstances, my decision was to go ahead with cremation. Maybe it was the weight of making and carrying through that process that did cause me to have (and remember) a dream. There was a furnace and fire involved in the dream, and Daddy's voice calling my name. However, after that one episode, there were other dreams in which my father appeared as a young, handsome, vital man…as he was during my growing up years. I do not remember the dreams as having any particular "storyline" but more of a feeling of Daddy's presence. When I would wake up, my reaction was a feeling of having had a pleasant memory. The first dream after he died is the only one which left me with a negative feeling, and it was not a lingering impression.

This dream seems to reflect cremation in the same way a dream about a coffin reflects interment. The dream uses the experience of the dreamer to convey the message that "It's really over." The suffering is over, and physical life has ended.

C. M. Parkes previously defined grief as the process of "making real" the fact of loss. We know intellectually that a person has died, but it takes time to incorporate this fact on a deeper level. Dreams help assimilate the loss on an emotional level, both consciously and subconsciously. By quickly changing the body into its natural elements, cremation makes it clear that life cannot continue as before.

Of course, there are social reservations regarding cremation. Cremation is a less traditional practice in Western culture. Also Mary DeLaine's father had changed his mind about following the original plan for his wife, which implied that he might have changed his mind about his own cremation. This was a difficult decision for a daughter to have to make; however, the circumstances left her few choices. Nevertheless, Mary might have been tormented by her first dream had she not had the pleasant dream experiences later. The later dreams of her father appearing healthy contributed to a reassuring outcome.

It is not unusual for the deceased loved one to speak or call out to the dreamer without appearing visually in the content of the dream. In her first dream experience after her mother's death, Katie heard her mother calling her but she didn't see her. We do not understand all the ways of dreams. I wonder if the manner in which dreamers take in information in their waking lives might not be a factor. Some people take information primarily through the visual channel, while others are more auditory. Mary DeLaine is a musician. She may be more likely to use the auditory channel, even in dreams, than many of us.

Delightful Dreams

Roger lived too far away from his parents to return home during his father's last illness. As a result, his father's caretakers received information and wisdom that Roger wished he could have been able to hear firsthand. He says, "In a dream my father appeared at a family gathering. He began dancing and held out his hand inviting me to join him. We danced a while. Then I woke up."

Roger's father was a good dancer and often danced at family gatherings. Happy memories of his father dancing were highlighted in his dream, which helped ease Roger's regrets at not being with him in his final days. Maybe the dream was also saying, "It's okay, it's time for some fun."

Comfort Offered by Departed Loved Ones

Peggy, a seminary student's wife, told me that when her mother died in Georgia, circumstances kept her away from the funeral. That night her mother appeared to her in a dream and said, "It's all right, Peggy."

Peggy's sharing of this comforting dream reminded me of the following story about another daughter who was comforted by her mother in a dream.

Jackie's mother was killed in a terrible shooting in Louisville, Kentucky. A mentally ill person walked into her workplace with an assault rifle and took eight lives before taking his own. Other people were left injured and permanently disabled. The whole community was shaken by the tragedy. Jackie's loss would have been painful under any circumstance because she and her mother were very close, but it was made especially acute by this senseless, mad killing spree. In her grief Jackie could hardly summon the energy to work and care for her children and her home. A year later, in a newspaper interview, Jackie reported that she had started to find relief when she began dreaming.

In one dream Jackie saw herself drive to a mall in a strange city. Once there, her two young daughters led her inside where her mother waited. Her mother, calm and beautiful, appeared younger than when she had died. No sorrow showed in her eyes. The two women embraced; Jackie cried inconsolably, but her troubled heart was soothed as her mother held her and let her cry and cry. She did not speak or try to stop the tears: "I woke up having been reassured by her. We were so close and she looked so good that it really relieved me" (Bryant et al.).

This dream not only consoled Jackie directly but it provided an outlet for crying and expressing grief. Dreams that comfort and reassure the bereaved are common. In this book you will find several dreams that provide a safe means of expressing grief.

After I had written these stories, a new mother shared a dream she had had the night of her mother-in-law's funeral.

Carol R. and her husband were students in Switzerland, a different continent from where they had grown up (South Africa, where their families still lived). Carol was four months pregnant when her husband's mother died unexpectedly. Only a few days before her death, they had spoken to her on the phone and announced the news that they were now expectant parents. The mother-in-law was not sick. Her last words, "Take care of that baby, Carol," did not seem unusual. Carol's doctor did not think it was wise for her to make the long flight with her husband for the funeral, so she did not. She gives the following account of her dream:

> The night of the funeral I saw Reuben's mother vividly in a dream, rather like a vision. I heard her speak the words again, "Take care of that baby, Carol."

Carol and her husband understood this to mean it was all right for her not to attend the funeral and that caring for the new life was more important.

The appearance of one's mother free from physical limitations is as comforting as direct words or actions. It is as if the mother is saying, "See, I'm fine now." My cousin Mary Lou shares this helpful dream that she had not long after her mother's death:

> She [Mother] was running, carefree-like, and was young—maybe twenties, and still had long hair, the curls I've seen in a few pictures of her at that age. She was laughing or smiling broadly—something I did not see her do much of the last ten or so years. The overwhelming impression was of a freedom, an ability to breathe easy— unfettered. The predominant color is green [and there are] fields with lots of sunshine, an overgrown field in deep July summer.

Aunt Katheryn, Mary Lou's mother, had been on oxygen, carrying a cumbersome oxygen tank with her everywhere. It was also difficult for her to get around after she had fallen twice. But she had a very independent spirit and she maintained her own home until she was nearly ninety. To see her through Mary Lou's dream, breathing and moving freely in the outdoors as when she had gardened in the sunshine, made me feel lighthearted. It gave me a pleasant memory of her. Sharing such dreams helps the dreamer and others as well; I urge you to be generous with your dreams.

Richard shares his experience of seeing his mother become progressively younger and stronger in a series of dreams. For several months these dreams centered on his inability to find and protect a lost and helpless young animal, often his collie as a puppy (who was no longer living) or his seventeen-year-old cat as a kitten. The searching behavior of the bereaved can be observed in this dream activity. Perhaps these dreams reflect his feeling of being unable to help his mother, who was crippled by arthritis and was in a wheelchair for the last years of her life. They may also depict the way he felt about himself after his mother's death, lost and helpless, even abandoned. When Richard's mother began to appear in his dreams, she would be in a serious or dangerous situation. He describes one of these dream situations:

> One dream involved our being on a jet airline flight together—something that never actually occurred. The plane flew into violent turbulence, which caused it to buck and dive. My mother was thrown to the floor and eventually trapped under shelving in the galley, from where I attempted to reach and extricate her.

The threatening dream situation gradually diminished. Even when some element of physical danger or risk remained, he would be able to reach, touch, and converse with her. Meanwhile, she grew stronger and younger, no longer confined to her wheelchair but walking first with a cane and then freely. In one of his final dreams in the series, he had this pleasant experience:

> We were again high in the mountains of northern New Mexico, where my family enjoyed many holiday trips when my brother and I were young. My mother was now hale and fit, and laughed again as she hauled buckets of water up a long hill from the stream or lake to the camping trailer.

Seeing his mother moving freely in a setting that aroused pleasant memories of both his parents (his father had died earlier) both reduced his grieving and indicated that he was working through his grief. At the end of more than a year of dreaming and grieving, it was clear to him that he had found greater peace.

The Management of Death and Dying

Virginia shared these dream experiences with me not long after her father's death:

> Dad had a stroke around Thanksgiving last year. He lived
> through it and was to have been discharged from the
> hospital. I was concerned because he was going to need
> skilled care. He already lived in a retirement home but he
> would need care and I didn't know how I could arrange
> it. I went to sleep thinking about this. As I went to sleep I
> heard, "You don't need to wrestle with that." The next
> morning the doctor called me at work and told me Dad
> had died in the night.

This dream is an *auditory* dream (a dream without a picture). Virginia was not quite asleep when it happened. Dreams that occur when the dreamer is between sleep and wakefulness are called *hypnogogic* dreams. Virginia's subconscious was preparing her for her father's impending death by suggesting that she need not burden herself with plans for his future.

This next dream underscored what had happened and helped her accept his death:

> After Dad died, he appeared to me. First, just his head,
> then his whole body sitting in a chair. He wore a suit he
> had worn in the forties with a gold pin in the lapel. He
> had regained his health. There were two persons with
> him that I think of as guides. One is a male. The other is
> a female, and she reminded me of Mary to whom the
> risen Jesus had said, "Don't touch me." Dad was smiling,
> and I asked her, "May I hug him?" We took a few steps
> toward each other and then we hugged. I felt the texture
> of his suit and the firmness of his body. The other guide
> said, "I am light, he is light. God is light." He guided Dad
> a few feet, and Dad said, "Take care of Mama." Then he
> was led toward the doorway. Dad said, "It's dark in
> there," to which the female guide replied, "Look, there is
> a golden light." Then the male guide led him into a

> tunnel. There were two doors. The male guide took Dad
> out one, and the female guide went out the other.
>
> The male guide was like a wise Ben Franklin. The
> female guide was like a good fairy in Cinderella. She
> protected Dad and gave permission to touch. She healed
> and comforted.

Virginia's father's appearance in a dream after his death is typical in several ways of other such dreams of bereaved persons. He is identified by his clothing and a pin. His health is restored. There is a strong sense of touch, giving texture to the fabric of his suit and the firmness of his body. The light, which is often a part of mourning dreams, is a comforting symbol of hope and promise, since God is the source of light.

In my experience guides do not appear often in dreams of the bereaved. There is a suggestion of one in Jean's dream (see chapter 2), in which there is a man she does not know and whose face she does not see, with her and her husband on a boat dock. Marie-Louise von Franz, a Swiss psychoanalyst, writes of "the guide of souls" who leads the dead into the beyond. She also says that the dreams of dying persons often contain the motif of "being fetched" by a relative or close friend (73). One certainty in Virginia's dream is that the guides represent assurance that her father is in wise and caring hands, which is comforting and healing to the dreamer.

Providing Closure to Acute Grief

My sister, Bea, dreamed about Daddy three years after his death. There is no set time for grieving to end according to grief specialists. Some grieving continues throughout life, but usually there is a time when acute mourning ceases. Bea's dream provided a closure to her acute grieving. Here is the dream as she told it to me:

> I'm helping Daddy to get packed. He'd been called up
> for the Persian Gulf war. In my dream I think it is so
> terrible for this to be happening to an old man. He
> seemed so sad. He is wearing a plaid robe that showed

his white legs below the hemline when he goes to get on the truck with all the other people. I run to where all of you are—to the house, I think it was. I say to all of you— you, Al, and Paul—"Let's go now and tell Daddy a final goodbye."

This dream occurred during the Persian Gulf conflict and seemed at first to be sending our father to war. Since he was not alive, Bea wondered what this could mean. When I asked her what the Persian Gulf meant to her besides a place of war, she said it was a place she knew very little about—a strange, mysterious, exotic place. Then I asked her, "And how is Daddy dressed? For war or for resting?" After discussing these questions, we concluded that the Persian Gulf represented death because of the war. Regardless of what else this dream meant, it was helping her say goodbye to Daddy.

Three years after the death of a parent may seem like a long grieving period. However, other circumstances in Bea's life may have added to her sense of loss and prolonged her grieving. Because of the age factor, we expect to give our parents to death eventually, and such a loss usually does not deprive us of as much as other losses do. One exception might be young adults in their twenties or thirties who have not yet achieved emotional independence, even though they may have achieved financial and physical separation.

One loss I feel keenly is the loss of a connection to the past—in other words, the documentation of my family history. One recent Christmas Mama documented a bit of my past with a gift. It was a tie rack made by my father. When I saw it, I remembered seeing it hanging on the wall when I was a child. Daddy had made it before I was born, while Mama made baby clothes for me. This was the way they spent their evenings in their little oil-field shack in Kansas. Daddy whittled the tie rack from a scrap of oil-field lumber. He didn't use glue or nails. Mama drew pictures of a man and a woman on it and then Daddy burned them into the wood. Mama's gift and its story to the family around the Christmas tree tied us to our parents' history and our background.

The Relationship of All Dreams
to the Loss of a Significant Person

My dreams about Daddy were not what I think of as typical grief dreams. That is, Daddy did not appear to me in a dream; although I did seem to be searching for him in a couple of them. In one, I am looking for him when he fails to come home. Another time, I am trying to reach him by phone. Both times, Mama is indifferent and preoccupied, and I think of the dreams as being more about Mama than about him.

My sister revealed that she also had dreams about Mama. Both of our dreams depicted Mama as behaving differently from the way we remembered her as children and still thought of her. We concluded that our dreams were helping us update our childhood views.

Nor were my dreams like my usual dreams. Immediately after Daddy died, my sister and I both had dreams of torture and suffering. We related these to Daddy's struggle and suffering. The doctor had told us that he was not without hope (we thought this was a mistake on the doctor's part). For this reason, Daddy thought he should work hard to live. We longed to tell him just to let go and let it happen. But we were afraid he would misinterpret this as meaning that we did not want him around any more, or that we just wanted to get it over with. He could be sensitive, and we did not want him to be in pain emotionally as well as physically.

It was not until a doctor at the hospital asked him if he wished to sign a paper not to be put on a ventilator that he stopped struggling and became more at peace. Still I was wondering if Daddy might have expected us to ask him not to sign it. He lived less than a couple of hours after that. My sister had been with him for most of his two-week hospital stay and much of the time during his earlier hospitalization.

Both times were torturous and stirred up bad feelings that she had stored away about herself. Her dreams at the time reflect this. In one dream she was looking for her red dress (one that she had actually had many years before). The dress made her feel good when she wore it. While she was looking for it, she was doused with water. She chanced to look in the mirror. She looked terribly forlorn, with her ugly, drab, brown clothing and her dripping hair. But she said to herself, "I *am* a good person." Then she found her red dress. She woke up feeling better.

My dreams were puzzling and differed from my usual dreams. Some time passed before I recognized that they were directed toward family dynamics.

In one early dream I was putting on boots with pockets around the legs. I was filling the pockets with supplies so I could fall behind enemy lines. I understood that I was to prepare to be a spy, so I asked myself, What does a spy do? The obvious answer—observe and gather information—did not help much. So I asked myself, Observe what? For what kind of information?

A month later I dreamed that, in some of Daddy's things, I found an envelope on which "P V T" was written in Daddy's handwriting. A word starting with "S" followed. I could not recall the word when I woke up. Maybe it was "secret" or "security." "P V T" might be an abbreviation for "private."

A couple of months later at Thanksgiving I had this dream:

> I am at our family home. Mama and I come across an attaché case. It holds unlaundered, but not noticeably soiled, clothing on top of some business papers. The clothes are a dark plaid flannel shirt and some dark socks. Mama says, "Oh, no, not more stuff to do something with." I respond, "That's all right, Mama, I'll take care of it," but she replies, "No, that won't be necessary."

I tried to understand this dream by looking at the objects. The attaché case represented business. Clothing is very representational of the person. These clothes identified the papers as Daddy's. That these clothes were unlaundered indicated that something of Daddy's had not been taken care of yet.

Dreams may also explain previous dreams. The envelope with "P V T" written on it came to mind. Both the envelope and the attaché case are containers for personal items.

Around the time I had this dream, I wanted to know about the insurance and taxes on our now jointly owned family farm.

Before Daddy died, he had left the farm to all four children with the stipulation that Mama live there as long as she desired. As part owner, I wanted to have a copy of the deed and to know about taxes and insurance. When I asked Mama, she told me that the boys look after it. Whatever was occurring was being done before Daddy died it seemed; and I thought we needed to share this responsibility in some way, each paying a fourth every year or taking turns annually. When I brought this up with my brothers, they told me not to worry. So that was it. "The girls" were being excluded—not intentionally, of course—from decisions about the farm which we now owned. In our family Daddy had always made the decisions and now the sons thought that they should fill in for him. But my sister and I wanted to be recognized as equal owners.

I had always lived a considerable distance from home and not able to get there often. When I did, I was more of a guest. Therefore, sometimes it may have appeared that I was not interested in the family business. Becoming one of the owners of the farm changed this. My dreams were making me realize that I needed to be involved.

Several people who were knowledgeable about real estate told me that whoever paid the taxes for seven years straight could claim ownership. I also talked with a lawyer friend about the appropriate manner of handling a joint ownership. He said that he knew, from personal and professional experience, this arrangement could cause difficulties within a family. He advised us to get together soon for an open discussion to work out any problems.

Mama was reluctant to discuss the situation, saying, "The boys are fair." My reply was, "But it's a matter of handling things correctly and legally so there is no confusion on the part of other family members." No doubt, our brothers thought they were doing us a favor by taking care of business and maintenance, but my sister and I did not want to be excluded from the business of our own property. Finally, about a year after Daddy's death, we did come together. (I give all of this background information because I think it has a bearing on the dreams that both my sister and I had during this interval.)

In one dream my sister felt the absence of Daddy's wisdom. In another, on the first night of a visit to Mama in our childhood home, Bea dreamed of being threatened by wild cats and chased by a wolf. She felt this hostile dream environment related to going home. Also, on my first night of a visit home, I dreamed of being escorted away by a man.

Such dreams depicted our feelings of not being included. The dreams were not comforting and did not appear to be related directly to the grieving process, but they were dreams of the bereaved. Possibly all of the dreams we have right after the loss of a significant person relate in some way to the loss. Perhaps, as part of the grieving process, the need for adjustment of family roles and responsibilities is brought to our attention by dreams.

I read a newspaper article by Lawrence M. Kutner that discussed what happens in sibling relationships when parents die. The following lines caught my attention and provided me with some understanding for my dreams:

1. They (adult siblings) may experience intense emotions as they evaluate the meaning of family and their roles within it.

2. Siblings must deal directly with each other without parents for mediators.

3. (Misunderstandings) "over who deserves what" are often as much a matter of symbolism (of the parent's affection) as of substance.

The circumstances or predicament in which the deceased person leaves the bereaved may make moving through the grief process difficult. Anger, even rage, about things that could have been and were not is natural. But if these feelings are held onto for too long, they can make us physically ill or we can become mired in chronic grief. Dreams can be a good resource for helping us resolve problems caused by such situations.

I have come across dreams of this nature in my reading. One of these dreams I found interesting because it, too, is a daughter's dream after her father's death. Jean and Wallace Cliff in *The Hero Journey in Dreams* write of a thirty-seven-year-old married professional woman whose dream was more than a rehashing of the unpleasant experiences of her father's dying (55-58).

The setting of the dream has the dreamer sailing on an old clipper ship. Other images included gray hair and a blueprint. The dreamer understood that the setting was connected with the subconscious, since water is often associated with the subconscious. So she reviewed the events of the previous day to try to determine what her subconscious might be trying to highlight.

The night before the dream she had been working at the unpleasant task of a budget when her sister phoned saying she feared that their family might be in a financial mess.

Memories surfaced from her subconscious about how money was dealt with in their family as she was growing up. Her father had been tightfisted, and her mother had given up autonomy for security. She and her sister had not done this; nevertheless, she still wanted to be her father's little girl and not worry about "dirty old money." By avoiding money problems, her family could stay close and not fight. But this approach was not working. Avoiding problems does not keep a family together. Even her own family's closeness was being threatened by this way of thinking. Her dream showed her that her parents' way of handling money was the cause of the mess her father had left and the source of her own problems with money.

A Three-Year-Old's Grandfather Visits Her in Her Sleep

Taylor was barely three years old when her grandfather died. She was deeply grieved and cried so much that even four months later her father's shirt was soaked with tears where he held her. Taylor had visited her grandfather weekly and she missed him. In addition, she became convinced that the angels were keeping him in heaven and would not let him come to her. However, on this dreary, drizzly January afternoon, she was a sparkling, happy little girl showing me her Christmas gifts and telling me about Paw-Paw. She mixed the two interests with no thought of one being of more importance than the other. Both were special to her.

"Paw-Paw called me Princess," she volunteered.

"What else can you tell me about Paw-Paw, Taylor?" I asked.

"Liked to eat grapes with me," she replied. This happy memory prompted her to ask her mother for some grapes, which she shared with me while her little dog watched. Her mother explained that the dog liked grapes, too. She and her Paw-Paw had included him in their grape-eating parties. We visited in this manner for a time, and then Taylor pulled her Christmas gift chair up in front of me and sat down, saying, "When I was asleep, Paw-Paw came to see me. He asked me how I was. He talked to me."

I asked her what they talked about. I couldn't be sure from her answer whether what they talked about was from her dream or from her memories of waking life with him. Perhaps it was a little of both.

Then with a thoughtful expression, she said, "I don't cry anymore." According to her parents this was so. In fact she seemed happy talking about him as though he were both present and gone.

Clearly, this sleeping experience was a dream that had helped Taylor to mourn and to be comforted. She was comforted to have parents who were receptive to her dream experience and encouraged her to talk about it and her Paw-Paw. It would have been easy to have discounted her experience because of her age and to discourage talk about her beloved Paw-Paw because his being gone had made her so sad.

I feel privileged to have been trusted with this most intimate experience from so young a child.

2. Dreams about Deceased Spouses

A series of dreams may help resolve grief by moving the bereaved through the mourning process. Initially, the survivor needs to accept the loss on both conscious and subconscious levels. Searching for the lost loved one may be an integral element of early dreams. This searching behavior may be accompanied by anger at being left alone and the secondary losses of safety and security. Finally, a common message that the departed seem to have for their loved ones and that seems to initiate the recovery process is to finish grieving and get on with living.

In this chapter I repeat the series of dreams used in the introduction. There I used them to describe dream categories according to the insights they offer. Here I use them to illustrate how dreams reflect the progression of healing in the grief process by taking you through the dreams of one bereaved dreamer.

Resolving Grief through a Dream Series

April's husband died of a heart attack suddenly and unexpectedly. There had been no indication of anything physically wrong with him. A series of dreams reflected her mourning process and helped her move through the worst of it. The first dream, which occurred immediately after his death, emphasizes the event itself. This dream moved her out of her initial shock and into feeling:

> I saw my husband, Orie, in a dream. He was wearing the navy suit he was buried in. He had his Gideon emblem pin on his lapel, and it was glowing like a light. He was sitting with a group of people. He smiled a dazzling smile at me and said, "I'm sorry I had to let you think I was dead." I felt so many mixed emotions. I was happy to see him, and yet I was almost angry because he didn't seem upset about leaving me. I wanted to stay with him, but the telephone rang and woke me up. For a long time after that I just prayed to God to let me at least see him in my dreams, but I didn't dream about him for a good while.

April knew her husband had died, but she had not had time to assimilate the information. Her husband's sudden death was totally incomprehensible; nevertheless, she knew in her dream that he had gone. He was wearing the suit in which he was buried. There was no doubt as to who he was, because he was wearing the emblem that represented the work that had been very dear to him, the work of the Gideon Bible Society. The emblem even glowed, as if to call April's attention to it and perhaps identify the spiritual significance of death. Orie was a successful businessman who volunteered his time on behalf of this organization. Since he was an excellent speaker, it would be natural for him to be with a group of people.

The group might also symbolize that death is a condition everyone must experience, that Orie was no exception, and that he was now with those who had already died. For Orie to be with people would also be natural for another reason; he always put himself at the service of others. This was a characteristic that April loved about him. For example, when my nephew was killed, Orie and April accompanied his family to another state for the burial.

Feelings are an important element in this dream—feelings that emerge from April's initial numbness. She described her emotions as mixed, but she did identify happiness, anger, and

2. Dreams about Deceased Spouses

longing. She was very happy to be with her husband even in a dream and longed to stay with him. Then she was angry when he was not concerned about leaving her.[1]

To be overwhelmed with so many feelings is chaotic and confusing; it drains the energy that is especially needed at this time. For a bereaved person to understand what he or she is feeling is painful as well, but it does release energy and move the person along in the grieving process.

Later, I read about a dream that reminded me of April's first dream. The dreamer was a young woman whose fiancé, also young, had just died of heart failure. In her dream she had received a letter from him in which he wrote how wonderful it was to follow a banner. He even drew a picture of the banner, which was blue with a crown and a fire under the crown. This banner symbolized her fiancé following his fate which was death; thus, she felt the banner had a spiritual significance. The most striking similarity to April's dream is that the young woman said, "On the one hand, I was happy about the letter, but on the other hand, I was sad and, above all, furious because he had left me..." and didn't seem to mind.

Verena Kast writes of this grief-stricken and furious young woman:

> The dream was instrumental in helping her to leave the
> first phase of mourning...the phase of absolute numbness
> that accompanied the denial that he had died. It brought

---

1 Incidents of the deceased not appearing concerned or sad about leaving loved ones are not uncommon in dreams. Several of the dreams in this book illustrate or suggest this. Dr. Marie-Louise von Franz had dreams of her father after his death in which "human warmth" seemed to have disappeared. She compares this to the "far away" and "detached" reaction observed with dying people (109). Perhaps death is not unlike other types of separations in which the person who separates does not grieve. For instance, a child who leaves home for school or a job or who runs away does not always feel sad. In a marital separation, the spouse who leaves may not feel the sadness that the remaining partner does. This is not always the way it is with separation in relationships, but what appears in dreams can also be observed in ordinary waking life.

her into the second phase of mourning, in which the
emotions of grief and anger could find expression (31-33).

I like Kast's explanation of the meaning of denial. She says
that numbness "cannot be seen only as repression of unpleasant
news," but as "reaction to an emotion too overwhelming to be
coped with" (54).

April's second dream contained the element of searching, a
characteristic of mourning associated with learning the painful
truth that her loved one was not there for her. In his book
Bereavement, C. M. Parkes discusses this searching behavior at
length. He does not consider such behavior aimless, because the
specific aim is to find the individual who is gone. The bereaved
person knows such a search is useless, but the urge to search is
so strong that she or he is not able to stop. This is especially so
of a mother whose child has died (62).

Dr. Joyce Brothers, an American psychologist, wrote that for
months after her husband died she would return home from a
trip expecting to see him when she walked into the apartment.
"I knew he would not be there, but there was always that tiny,
crazy glimmer of hope that he would be," she explained (230-33).

Sometimes this searching behavior takes the form of looking
for something to do. For example, April went window-shopping
in the malls with friends. This "looking around" was perhaps a
form of searching.

In addition to searching behavior, this next dream is concerned
with physical safety. Safety and security were secondary losses
that occurred when April's husband was no longer there for her.
Secondary losses can invoke great fear.

Of this dream she says, "I still don't know for sure it wasn't a
vision; it was so vivid." Often this is the way the bereaved
experience dreams of their dead loved ones.

> I was looking under the bed, checking as I always did in
> closets and in the house when I came back in from being
> out. I was on my knees looking under the bed, and
> when I straightened up, arms went around my waist from
> behind. I looked down at the arms and thought, Oh,
> good, it's Orie. Then I looked over my shoulder, and

there was Orie's face. For just a second I was so happy.
Then a voice that seemed to come from inside me said,
"No, no! It's not Orie! It just looks like him." This terrible
fear started at the top of my head and went to my feet.
I've never been so frightened in my life. I remembered
what I had been taught and said, "In the name of Jesus,
get out!"

She said that when she awoke she read the Bible and prayed
all night, and for a long time she did not want to see her husband
in a dream. This dream confronted her with the fact that Orie
was not physically present to keep her safe. It made her realize,
from deep inside her whole being, that she was alone. The time
had come for April to rely on her own resources and make a life
for herself, probably something she had never before considered.
Orie had managed all the family business. April had never so
much as written a check for household or personal expenses,
let alone handle investments and insurance. To think that she
had to learn about and be responsible for the finances, when
she was least able to cope emotionally, was terribly frightening.
April was filled with fear from head to toe. Even in her dream
she did as she had been taught in waking life—she prayed. She
invoked the name of Jesus as though she were exorcising a
demon and commanded fear to get out. After waking up, April
sought relief from this overwhelming fear by praying and reading
the Bible, and she was strengthened.

Indeed, April did not meet her husband in a dream for a long
time, not until she had come to the place where she had some
confidence in her ability to manage an ongoing life.

About a year later April and my sister came to visit me. April
became sick with what she thought was a stomach virus. She
went to bed to take a nap and, feeling cold, pulled the covers
over her. Although she did not dream about her husband, she
connected the following dream with the previous ones about Orie:

I dreamed the door blew open. This frightened me. Then
I saw there was a storm with both dust and hail in it. I
thought, That doesn't mix. As I awakened I thought of
my children, Were they okay?

April's concern for safety and security surfaced again in this dream. And something else is going on—a storm with elements that do not mix (an inner conflict?). We were in the midst of a hot, dry summer, and she went to bed in an air-conditioned room. So it is easy to determine the source of the image (a storm with both dust and hail). The question is, What is this image depicting in her life? What is it that does not mix?

We discussed what April was doing at the moment. She was having a pleasant time with friends. Could she have been feeling ambivalent about enjoying herself or about going on with her life while she was grieving? Did she feel the two didn't mix?

Something else very positive developed with this dream. April woke up concerned for her children. Her children are grown; however, they may have had needs, especially with their grief, that she had not been aware of or emotionally able to help with because of her own intense grief. April's dream reflects that she was becoming aware of them. Concern for the living is one indicator of readiness to move on into life. This dream appears to be opening the door for April to do just that, for it begins with the door blowing open. This does not mean she would not continue to miss her husband and experience pangs of grief. But grief, with all its difficulties, was becoming more manageable so she could begin to attend to other areas of her life.

Although April was disturbed by this unusual dream, it was really showing her that she was healing. Dreams often exaggerate to get the dreamer's attention; usually, the results of the dream are not as serious as the dreamer expects. Opposites expressed by the dust and hail, as well as a storm in the midst of some pleasure, indicate healing. A characteristic of dreams is that they bring oppositional forces together, which promotes wholeness (healing).

About three years after April's husband died, she had a dream that left her feeling happier instead of bereft as after her first dreams. She writes this fourth dream in a letter:

> I was in a motel room with some children (I think they
> were my grandchildren) and my daughter, Joy. I went
> into the hall across from us and found two blonde-haired

women who had been killed. I ran back into our room
trying to hide what had happened from the children, as
they wanted to go out. I told Joy what happened, and we
had hamburgers brought in for the children. I looked out
the door and there was Orie and a policeman putting a
cover over the dead girls. I felt so much love in my heart
and thought, That's just like Orie, taking care of
everything for me. I felt his protection again, and it felt so
good. In my dream he came and sat down at the table
with me. I saw that lock of hair that always fell down on
his forehead, and I reached over and brushed it back. I
felt very happy—like old times. I woke up right after that.
I felt more at peace after this dream.

Some might label this a wish-fulfilling dream. But, looking at
it in the context of the previous dreams and the dreamer's life, I
see that the dreamer has made some discoveries in this dream.
The dream depicts her looking after herself and her remaining
loved ones as Orie had looked after her, and it feels good to her.

I did not go into the dream imagery with April, because it is
usually better to let the bereaved dreamer feel the impact of the
total dream experience as I listen to the dream. This dream is full
of meaningful images, so I am yielding to the temptation to give
my impressions here. There is the image of the women being
covered. They may represent aspects of April, such as helpless-
ness and naïveté, that died in the grieving process. Orie's death
protected her from dependency, which until now she had not
felt, and made it necessary for her to grow in ways she needed.
The dream also shows April that she is a very resourceful person.

Another aspect of this dream is that April is able to experience
and even enjoy her deceased husband as part of her life again—
although in a different sort of a relationship—and then leave him
again and awaken without feeling so sad. Her dream helped her
remember the way his hair fell, and she felt more at peace
afterward. As the French novelist Marcel Proust (1871-1922)
writes, "Memory nourishes the heart, and grief abates."

Even the setting in a motel indicates that a change is taking
place in April's life; she has moved out into the world. The

dream's use of her daughter Joy instead of another child is significant in further setting the tone of happiness used to describe her meeting with Orie. It may also be that the daughter-named-Joy refers to feeling joyful that their marriage existed and realizing that even death cannot take away the fact that their lives were spent together.

April still has times of sadness and feelings of grief, but she can allow them to surface and let them go. She writes, "God is healing me, but every time I come home from a trip I feel weepy. There are times when something hits me like a blow and I cry, but then I bounce back and go on." Somehow, without her understanding how much, her dreams help her accept the full impact of her loss on both the unconscious and conscious levels and build a life of her own.

The Departed's Common Message

Jean's dream of her deceased husband conveys this common message:

> Maurice, my husband, and I, and some man I didn't know—I didn't see his face—were standing at a boat dock waiting to be rescued from high water. The waves were big and water was rising rapidly. Along came a small boat to rescue us. The boat was crowded and there was only room for one to get on board. Maurice was putting me on the boat. He would not let me stay there with him. I couldn't understand why we couldn't make room for one more. But I reluctantly got on the boat, and he waved to me as we left to board a large ship somewhere. I knew that was the end for him. I didn't know any of the people on the boat.

Jean's husband had cancer. As with most cancer deaths, he suffered much physical and psychological pain. This dream emphasizes his death and confronts her with the need to live her life without him.

The image of rapidly rising water pictures how overwhelmed (drowned) she feels in her sadness and in the business matters that accompany a husband's death. With some discussion Jean understood that her husband was actually saying it was time for her to move on into the ebb and flow of life by putting her on a rescue boat filled with people. The boat would take her to the ship and get her back on the course of living. Grief tends to isolate; her dream was saying that the time for such isolation was over.

Jean was reluctant to let go of her life with her husband. His waving goodbye told her that it really was the end of their life together, as she had known it. In other words, they had to part.

This dream helped Jean accept her husband's death and start a new life's journey of her own. Another way of saying this, according to Ann Faraday, a pioneer in contemporary dream research, would be that the most common message of the departed in the dreams of the bereaved is to ask them to stop grieving. She relates a dream in which a woman dreamed her dead mother was drowning in a pool. She said, "Daughter, these are the tears you have shed for me. Let me go for I am drowning in them" (274-75).

Verena Kast discusses this separation factor involved in the grieving process in her book, *A Time to Mourn*. She believes dreams help the bereaved dreamer achieve separation and she illustrates with a dream that I will paraphrase here.

The dreamer and her husband are together on a train with other passengers. At a certain place everyone must climb out— except her husband. The dreamer appeals to the "highest authority" to continue with her husband "but to no avail." They say goodbye tenderly. She feels numb as she tries to find a returning train. She searches endlessly, running from train to train, all night long. At last she finds herself on a train going back with a lot of people. She is very much afraid (264).

The element of searching is often found in the dreams of the bereaved. Searching and running from train to train pictures the dreamer's effort to get her life back on track. The dream is also reporting to her that she is able to go on living in the world despite her fear of facing new circumstances. Although she was disturbed by this dream, she later pointed to it as being very important to her recovery.

Anger is a part of grief. As Jean told her dream, I thought I detected a bit of anger at Maurice's sending her out to face life alone. After we talked about the dream, Jean seemed to be comforted by the feeling that her husband was helping (rescuing) her through her dream. I let her focus on this good feeling. Anger is a normal reaction to death and sometimes needs to be dealt with. Dreams can invite us to work through issues that may be the cause of our anger and resentment.

One technique of dealing with this anger is to have a waking conversation with the deceased. This can be done privately or with the guidance of another person. It is also helpful to voice negative as well as the positive thoughts and feelings in expressing our goodbyes to the deceased. We can say, "I'll miss (what we will miss about the deceased)," and "I won't miss (whatever we didn't like)."

In Jean's case I did not think it was necessary to bring up the anger. It is usually better to move slowly with our dreams, savoring the good feelings that working with them brings and dealing with other feelings when they persist. If there indeed was anger, it apparently did not become a serious difficulty.

Jean later wrote, "I dreamed of Maurice last night, but it didn't disturb me. We were just talking with some friends." These later dreams bring to mind *Necessary Losses* by Judith Viorst, in which she says, "through mourning we let the dead go and we take them in." We let go of their flesh-and-blood presence, but we take them in "by making them a part of what we think, feel, love, want, do—we can both keep them with us and let them go" (249).

Climbing Stairs to Visit the Deceased

Mama dreamed of climbing stairs to visit Daddy after his death. Our Missouri farmhouse had stairs leading to bedrooms and to the basement. The imagery might have come from that; however, stairs appear in other people's dreams involving the departed.

About two and one-half years after my father died, Mama had a dream that she describes as different from her usual dream pattern. She begins with some background and continues into the dream:

It goes back a few years when your Dad and his friends, Bill Wells and Joe Warnol, worked as carpenters and stayed away from home through the week. In the dream Verna Wells and I went to visit them. (I don't know where they are.) We had to go up a lot of steps to their room. We met your Dad at the top of the stairs. He was dressed in pants, jacket, shirt and tie, and I asked him, "What kind of a job do you have that you are dressed like that?" (This question about clothes stems from the fact that he worked as a carpenter and wore carpenter overalls on the job.) He said, "Come into the room and I'll tell you, but be quiet, that man is sleeping." The dream ended there with no hint as to who the sleeping man was.

Mama did not think of Daddy as no longer living in this dream, but there seemed to be that implication since Bill and Joe are no longer alive either.

An interesting facet to this dream is that the dreamer is going to the deceased one instead of the deceased coming to the dreamer. Still, her deceased husband appears to her in the dream. To me, this illustrates how flexible and completely free dreams are in putting together the content of their dramas.

Climbing stairs may represent going to a higher level (heaven?) or trying to accomplish a goal (living through her grief and with her loss?).

There is also an element of surprise in finding her husband wearing dress-up clothes instead of work clothes and in her discovering that the circumstances are different. This suggests that his death was not yet a reality on the emotional level. Acceptance does not come all at once, but in spurts and pieces (Evans). [2]

The sleeping man is the most mysterious part of Mama's dream. Dreams are not allegories, nor are they documentaries. For me, there is a touch of humor here, and I could not resist

---

2 Christopher Evans, a psychologist, tells about giving up smoking and dreaming about it several times long after he felt it was a reality. It is as though time is required to process the information on all levels of awareness.

asking Mama, "Would you have wanted it to be a sleeping woman?" Actually, could this have been the dream's way of having Daddy say he just wanted to converse with Mama in a dream while everyone was sleeping? Mama did not say but she may have wished that she could see Daddy and talk with him. If so, this would have been a lovely wish-fulfillment dream.[3]

Mama had another dream in which she was climbing many stairs with no effort at all. Perhaps this dream was helping her realize that living with grief was getting easier. Possibly it reflected her physical condition of being more rested than when she cared for Daddy while he was ill. It might also mean that she felt spiritually strengthened to get through the task of grieving. I do not think all these meanings have to be identified for the dreamer to benefit from them. Similarly, we do not have to understand all about the digestive process when we eat food for it to give us health and energy.

However, in Mama's third dream, climbing stairs took more effort and she said, "This is just too much work. I'm not going to do this." This dream, therefore, seems to contradict the second dream, and we did not know what to make of it at the time. Now I think it may be saying that she was finding grief tiring and taking too much energy, and she was ready to be through with it.

---

3 Mama died as I completed this manuscript. In her things we found the following note, which she had written in response to this dream visit. This is the first time I knew about this very private communication. Did she feel self-conscious writing to her dead husband? Rather, I think it indicates just how personal this time between the dreamer and the dreamed is—a time to ponder and to cherish.

"Dear husband,
   How wonderful you looked last night when I saw you as I dreamed. What joy to hear your voice again with the same old love. In a way it makes me lonely for your memory is so clear. But come again, my dear, it makes you seem so near."

3. Dreams about Deceased Siblings

Young children who experience the death of a sibling can be deluged with guilt, especially if they are close in age. However, few books have been written about the particular grief of an adult for a brother or sister. The sister-sister relationship is particularly intense and we will explore it later; but I have found no accounts of dreams that picture the feelings of brothers' losing a sibling. Neither have I found a brother who is willing to share such a dream.

Dealing with Multiple Losses

Dreams helped Patty through the agonizing grief of multiple deaths. A trained nurse, Patty was in commercial real estate at the time she shared this dream. First, she told me about her family. Her sister, Dorothy, had died of cancer in 1971. The next year, her brother was hit by a car and died. There was only a year's difference between her and her sister; her brother was four years younger. There were seven children in the family.

One surviving brother, in responding to his grief, seemed to be angry at Patty, as if he were afraid she too might be taken and he would be hurt again. Another brother and a sister seemed to withdraw from her. Patty felt abandoned.

Patty and Dorothy had been devoted sisters. But their closeness in age may have made Patty resent sharing her mother with Dorothy. This possibility occurred to Patty because, when her sister died, she discovered herself thinking, Now I won't have to share my mother anymore. This made her feel very guilty.

Patty had not finished grieving for Dorothy when her brother was tragically killed, adding sudden grief to incomplete grief. After his death she began having horrible dreams of tornadoes, storms, spiders, and snakes. Patty does not recall that she associated these dreams with the deaths at the time; however, looking back she feels they depicted her feelings of distress over the deaths of her sister and brother. She dreamed of her brother "that he was dug up and cremated. Although this seemed to be a bad dream at the time, Patty thinks it may have helped her accept the reality of his death; because of the condition of her brother's body, the casket had been kept closed. Sometimes not being able to view the body before burial makes accepting the death more difficult.

Patty could not bring herself to share these troubling dreams with her husband. The time came when she described herself as "going off the deep end." With her husband's encouragement, Patty consulted her pastor who worked with her on her grief for about four months. During this time the nightmares ceased, but she still felt troubled. Her pastor encouraged her to face her brother and sister in her mind and talk with them as though she could actually see them. She could do this with her brother, but not with her sister. She said she would yell and scream that she could not.

One night Patty went to bed in deep despair. She even thought about how she might die, because it was the only way she could see her sister. That night she had the following dream:

> In my dream I woke up in a room filled with smoke. It was hazy like a fog. My children, Steven, Penny, and Pam, were with me. They were little—younger than seven, eight, and nine, their real ages. I picked Penny up and sat her on the counter. It was a circular counter. Then, I missed Steven. I started hollering for him. Then a

voice came from a cloud saying, "It's all right," and I saw
my sister. She looked well, just as she had before her
illness, except her four front teeth were missing. (She had
lost these teeth and had permanent dentures in their
place.) I exclaimed, "Dorothy, I thought you were dead!
Where is Steven?" She answered, "Steven has been
revived and has returned to earth. You're going to
heaven—all of you—Pam and Penny, too. I've come to
help you."

I tried to touch her and she said, "Don't touch me,
you're not yet dead." "Dorothy, can't I just talk to you?" I
asked. Then she reached out and touched me on the
shoulder with a firm but gentle shove and said, "It's going
to be all right." It was Dorothy who touched me, but I
felt as if it was the hand of God gently pushing me back
into life.

I woke my husband, who was sound asleep on the far
side of the bed and told him the dream. It couldn't have
been my husband who touched me. He was too far away.

A child's need can break through the haze of a parent's
depression and get attention. This is like a sleeping parent who
is not awakened by most noises but is tuned in to the baby's cry.
Patty explains her dream this way: In the midst of her despair
the children were reminding her that she had a responsibility to
the living, and in a way, they served as a contact with her sister
who came to her offering to help her.

Discussing the missing teeth, Patty said she had never seen
Dorothy without her teeth although she herself had worked for
a dentist. To her the dream presented her sister without the
dentures to say, "There is no fakery here."

Patty interprets the gentle push as God pushing her back into
life through her sister's touch. The appearance of a loved one as
a spiritual being of comfort and encouragement is characteristic
of dreams that reflect the beginning of the dreamer's recovery.
A part of Patty had died with her sister and this had affected her
children, too. The dream brought her back to life and to care for

her children and others who needed her. It helped her get on with her life.

Patty stated, "This dream is as vivid now as it was when I dreamed it sixteen years ago." Since then she has had pleasant dreams about her sister.

With so many losses close together, it is no wonder that Patty suffered an emotional overload: disbelief, sadness, abandonment, guilt, and ambivalence. However, her dreams helped her move through her grief in an extraordinary way.

Patty was very observant to recognize that her dreams depicted her swirling feelings as tornadoes and storms with threatening creatures. Dreams do picture feelings. The dream of her brother helped her accept the reality of her brother's death by providing the body. A natural urge to deny his death was reinforced when she was deprived of seeing his body. So, with no evidence of her brother's body, the funeral ritual did not help promote acceptance of his death. Memories of receiving the condolences of friends and acquaintances, viewing the body of the loved one with others and in privacy, and seeing the casket at the grave help confirm the reality of the loss later. This is so even when the grieving person is still emotionally unable to accept the death.

Patty's dream used the image of cremation to dispose of the body instead of the traditional burial that had occurred. This conveyed to her that her brother's life as she had known it had ended. By quickly changing the body into natural elements, cremation makes it clear that the person's life cannot continue as before.[1]

Siblings and Grief

To discuss the particular grief of an adult for a sister or brother will help us understand this factor in Patty's grief. Until I discovered *Grieving: How to Go on Living When Someone You*

---

1 "[Cremation] can facilitate mourning by effectively symbolizing the finality of the relationship you had with the deceased and suggesting life must go on without that person" (Rando 275).

Love Dies, I had not found a book that dealt with the death of a brother or sister in adult life. The author, Therese A. Rando, writes, "There is no loss in adult life that appears to be so neglected as the death of a brother or sister" (225). Later I found another discussion about the loss of a brother or sister in a book entitled *Necessary Losses* by Judith Viorst.

The problem of guilt can be intense for a young child when a sibling dies, especially when they are close in age. I have observed this even in older college-age brothers when one died in an accident and the other survived. Sometimes the guilt comes because the survivor believes she or he caused the death, either in reality or by wishing it. At other times the guilt comes because the survivor thinks the deceased sibling was a better person and more deserving of life. Quite often feelings conflict. Patty experienced such emotions when she thought to herself, Now I won't have to share my mother anymore. This innate competition among siblings for parental attention and love is a normal development that carries on into adulthood. Surviving siblings can come to see that this conflict is as inevitable a part of life as affection and loyalty.

Viorst identifies these conflicting feelings as "triumph and guilt"—triumph at getting rid of a rival, guilt about the wish to get rid of the rival, sorrow at being bereft of a playmate (260). She shares a memory of a time when her family was taking a trip on an ocean liner. Her two-and-a-half-year-old sister disappeared. The ship was searched and she was not found; so the family became convinced that she had drowned. She describes the mixed emotions she felt from thinking that this had happened because of her dearest and darkest wish to be rid of her little sister. "Oh, what horror! Oh, what guilt! And oh, what Joy!" (261).

Another factor that may have contributed to the intensity of Patty's grief is the sister-sister relationship. The slight age difference between the two sisters appears to have contributed to their close bond. Despite the guilt of normal sibling competition in which she feels she won her mother's total attention, Patty also feels the pain of loss.

In her book *Sisters,* Elizabeth Fishel presents case histories that explore this special bond. Fishel found that "from birth to death, sisters model and pattern their lives on each other. They take cues from each other....channels of communication are often more open and accessible, less guarded and defended against than lines between parent and child" (64-65).

In families with several girls, it is not unusual for two sisters to form a closer relationship with each other than with the others. Age, temperament, shared rooms, interests, and other factors all play a part. Later, according to Fishel, other experiences—geography, lifestyle, adulthood work and politics, marriage and child rearing— may change this bond or continue it. Also, surviving sisters may lose their will to live after one of them is gone (Fishel 164).

This can be true of brothers as well. When my father died at age eighty-two, his brother, eleven years younger, died two-and-a-half months later. Although he had been in poor health, his death had not been expected so quickly.

Brothers have not shared dreams of a deceased sibling or their feelings regarding a brother or a sister with me, nor do I recall reading such stories. In fact, I may be idealizing the sister-sister relationship because the sisters I know—my mother and her sisters, my father's sisters, and other sisters with whom I'm acquainted—have strong attachments. However, I cannot resist including the following stories, which I think help explain why Patty felt so grieved after the loss of her sister.

Recently, I have read two articles on the intensity of the sister-sister relationship. In a newspaper article entitled, "Sisters Are Like Shadows of Our Other Selves," the writer, Rheta Grimsley Johnson, tells the story of a sister's sharing a kidney with her older sister. She describes her own sister:

> She was always a tough little cuss, a tomboy more prone to action than words.
>
> The two of us spent hours on horseback._ I rode the cooperative quarter horse in front. Sheila trailed like a dinghy on the aptly named pony, Rebel.
>
> She had a Buster Brown haircut and perpetually skinned knees and the most determined personality I've ever affronted. Rebel ran her through ponds, low limbs, and barbed wire.

> But when I checked, she was always somewhere back
> there (Johnson A9).

Johnson concludes, "Sisters are nature's blessing and curse, our refuge and challenge, our best friend and our worst enemy. But when you check, they're always somewhere back there" (A9).

The other article was in *Woman's Day* magazine. Entitled "When I Found My Sister, I Found Myself," it also illustrates the uniqueness of this special relationship. Two sisters had been separated at ages four and two and grew up in adoptive families. When they were separated, the older one cried and cried for her baby sister. Although the younger one did not remember having a sister, she always felt something was missing. She tried to fill the void with drinking and bingeing. After twenty-four years the sisters were reunited; and together they searched for and found their older half-sister (Ivey).

The sister bond shows up in the dreams and stories of every culture I've investigated. I found the following example in a study of African dreams. Rosemary Chikaili, age thirty-three with a seventh-grade education, teaches Sunday School in her church. She says:

> I just always dream about my elder sister....She died in
> 1984. She was 35 years old. I was very close to her. She
> comes and goes away without looking at me. I don't feel
> anything during or after the dream. I have these dreams
> many times (Hayashida, *Significance of Dreams*, 291).

Elidah Phiri, age thirty-three and married, is a member of the International Baptist Church where she sings in the choir. She had a series of dreams involving snakes and dead people. Her deceased sister appeared in two of these dreams. The dreams were rather perplexing to her. She could not say what they meant except that the snakes represented Satan. Since the sister was helping her, I wonder: Is her sister's presence intended to give her courage in the face of some difficulty in her life, perhaps something she considers evil? One of the dreams follows:

> In 1980, when I was expecting my last born, I had a
> dream in which I was chased by snakes. I ran very fast

but those snakes were faster than me so I started flying. After flying for some time, I got tired and fell in water. Just then my late sister came, got hold of my hand, and swam across the water before the snakes caught up with me (Hayashida, *Significance of Dreams,* 401).

Greeting card companies recognize the sister-sister bond. My sister once sent me a card with a poem entitled, "My Sister…My Friend." In it the poet conveys the message that her sister is the one who has laughed and cried with her, understands her, and is always there for her.

Joyous Dreams

One of the ways dreams can deal with the management of grief is by giving us memories to enjoy. Such dreams found elsewhere in this book include Joyce Brothers's "miracle" dream, Anne Brooks's "real" dream, the *Guideposts* writer's "joyful" dream (chapter 6), and the dream of the little boy's time with his beloved grandfather (chapter 5).

In her article "Joyful Dreams," psychologist and dream specialist Gayle Delaney says dreams of joy are to be appreciated as fully as possible and that "before we take the important step of seeing how it informs our waking experience, we should really listen to the dream and relive it…allow the dream to linger with us and we with it." These dreams "offer us the sweet nectar of life and thus fortify us in this sometimes difficult enterprise of life" (1). I think we naturally savor dreams of joy in bereavement despite their bittersweet quality. Certainly they are fortifying.

My three-and-one-half-year-old sister, Helen, who had died and been buried on Easter Sunday, appeared to me in a joyous dream. She was buried in a light blue taffeta dress trimmed in pink with a tiered, gathered skirt and puffed sleeves. The white blossom of an Easter lily had been placed in her hand. Not long afterward I saw her in a dream. She was wearing the same dress, carrying the Easter lily, and walking down the road toward our home on a beautiful sunny morning. She was well and smiling, and I woke up feeling comforted. I was only ten years old then, and I have very few vivid memories of her. This is one memory and it is the way I most remember her.

I cannot remember any of the dresses Helen wore while she was living, but I remember the one in which she was buried. It is interesting how often loved ones appear in dreams wearing the clothes in which they were buried (as seen also in April's dream of her husband). One elderly woman I know, whose husband died many years ago, remembered the dream she had soon after his death. He was wearing the tweed suit in which he had been buried. She also remembered the color of it and the feel of its texture.

4. Dreams about Deceased Children

Children should outlive their parents. When children die, we mourn not only their loss but the loss of their future and our future with them. The loss of a child is an enduring grief, which can remain long after the acute stage of mourning eases. Holidays, birthdays, anniversaries, and special events can trigger mourning long after the death has occurred. Often, however, dreams help parents assimilate the fact of their children's loss and eventually come to accept it.

Dream Visits Ease Emptiness and Longing

To outlive your child is untimely, unnatural, and unthinkable for most parents. Children are meant to grow up and live longer than their parents. Grief for a child is enduring. Sigmund Freud, on what would have been his dead daughter's thirty-sixth birthday (she had died ten years previous), wrote to a friend that, although he knew the acute stage of mourning subsides, he would remain inconsolable.

Patsy and Reid were confronted with this most distressing of all griefs. Patsy writes the following description of her dream:

A Morning Dream Visit

Within a couple of weeks after the death of our nine-and-a-half-year-old son (resulting from a chronic illness), I had a dream in which he appeared to me.

I was in bed as I actually was at the moment and he walked into the room and up to the bed beside me. This was almost thirty years ago—1966—and I am not sure now if words were spoken or not. It seems as if there were but I don't remember any. The vision of him, I remember very clearly.

The most unique thing about this "dream visit" was the sense of having the feeling of gnawing emptiness and longing for him assuaged, resulting in a very comforting and fulfilled feeling, almost as if a heavy weight was removed and replaced with something soft and cozy. This [last sentence] is more of an after-the-fact description.

I had never heard of anyone telling of dreaming this sort of dream so I didn't share it for many years, which probably accounts for possible memory loss of any spoken words. A few years ago I read a newspaper article that stated this was a common occurrence [and I] shared my experience with Lois.

Holiday Dreams

Evelyn, my father's cousin, experienced the death of two daughters at different times. Her husband found it very difficult to accommodate to the loss, especially at Christmas, which placed an added burden on Evelyn. Her whole life had changed, but she managed to find comfort in the things that do not change, such as Christmas traditions. (Individual differences in grieving behavior may complicate this process.)

At Christmastime, many years after her daughter Carol's death, Evelyn had the following dream: "I dreamed of Carol being home for a holiday from college. I felt peaceful when I awakened."

Evelyn's dream gave her a pleasant memory of Carol from a time before her illness. The dream not only gave her peace at a stressful time but it confirmed that she had reached the stage in her mourning where she could cope with ongoing life and also be enriched by memories of her daughter.

Holidays, anniversaries, and family events can intensify grief reactions for many years after the death event and even after grief has subsided. To experience an upsurge of grief at these times is a normal reaction. Dreams bear witness to the truth of the saying, Once bereaved, always bereaved; although sometimes dreams make these special times more bearable.

Dreams Bring Acceptance of Death

My Aunt Neva, a grandmother in her eighties, showed unusual insight into the meaning of her dream in which her grandson appeared after his death. She described her dream as follows:

> One dream I had I'm sure God gave to me for comfort. I
> was unable to really believe it [her grandson's death]. I
> felt like I was in a bad dream. Then one morning early, I
> dreamed I got out of bed and was looking out the front
> door. A pickup truck came down the hill and stopped,
> and Gilbert got out. I started running toward him, saying,
> "Oh, Gil, I knew it was a dream!" And he said, "Hello,
> Gramma." I held out my arms and he disappeared. I
> woke up, cried and cried, and that was the last time. That
> was God telling me to accept it.

This is a good example of a dream that helped the dreamer assimilate the information that her grandson was dead. In chapter 1, Aunt Neva's daughter gives her experiences of her mother's dying. Gilbert (the grandson in the above dream) and three other grandsons who had died enter into these dreams. Although Aunt Neva had nine children, many grandchildren, great-grandchildren, and even great-great grandchildren, they were all very dear to her, and she felt their loss keenly.

Another Person's Dreams May Bring Comfort

Receiving comfort through the dreams of others was my sister's special gift when her son died. These dreams are about my nephew, Gary, at the time of and after his death in December 1971.

After my sister's seventeen-year-old son, Gary Simmons, was killed in a car accident, the mother of one of his friends handed her a white folder that contained a handwritten account of the following experiences related to Gary and his death:

> Jean, I would like to share with you, Lee, and your family some of my experiences concerning Gary.
>
> From the very first time I met Gary, it seemed as though he was someone very special…. Gary was always a thoughtful boy…. The last time I saw him was on Sunday morning, December 5th. He said he and Robbin and some of the other kids would come over one evening that week.
>
> On the afternoon of this tragedy (December 9), I was grocery shopping at Montesi's and just suddenly I felt sick, or depressed—strange, and that I must get home. That was approximately 3:30 P.M. I immediately went to the check stand. As I started to leave the store, I asked a lady for the time, and she said it was 3:40. I just couldn't get to the car fast enough. I hesitated to go by the library on Raines and Barton to check in some overdue books, but the traffic was very heavy at that time, which I thought was due to the rainy weather. I stopped by the library, and went on down to the shopping center on the way back to exchange a Christmas item. I still felt I *must* get home.
>
> I proceeded down 51, and then saw the wreck. It must have been 4:30 by that time. When I saw the demolished cars, I immediately started crying and, though I discovered later there was no resemblance, I first thought "Simmons' Car," referring to the dark-colored car—why, I still don't know. There was a lot of traffic, and I couldn't see too well. Immediately after reaching home, I called

Mrs. Owens, a friend of mine in the complex, and asked her if she had heard about the wreck, who was in it, and told her of my thoughts, etc. I told her I felt strongly it was the Simmons' [car]. Approximately fifteen minutes later, Mrs. Russo called and said Gary was killed. I honestly thought I would just die—a boy so gifted, such talent, so happy, so well-loved by all who knew him—a boy who was in our home many times—a boy who was always so grateful when I drove him to summer school. When he and Randy would spend the night with Don, we would have a good breakfast before church— scrambled eggs, bacon, hot biscuits and gravy. He would say, "Gravy for breakfast?" But, soon he would be reaching for the bowl a second time. We always had a good laugh about that....

When the accident happened and his picture appeared in the paper, many people whom I did not know well, who lived in this complex, knocked on my door asking if this was the boy (Gary) who went swimming out here this past summer with Don. And they spoke of his being such a happy boy....

I was so touched by this great loss that by Friday night, December 10th, I struggled for rest and peace. When I finally drifted off to sleep, I dreamed I was in heaven, it seemed. What a beautiful, immaculate street I was walking on, with such radiant light—such magnificent beauty! Unexplainable—no words exist to describe the beauty—such luscious colors, the most beautiful grass and flowers (perfect, spotless). I saw animals, spotless, in such luscious colors and even beautiful radiant frogs along the roadside. Then suddenly from somewhere a voice said, "Hi." I could see no one. I said, "Who are you?," and he said, "I'm Gary, and I will have a new body, and I have a new life." His voice sounded so happy. I awoke with my arms stretched out reaching for him. It had been so real.

Saturday night, December 11th, I was so disturbed after being at the funeral home that afternoon. When I fell asleep, I saw Gary come down through the ceiling looking just as he did at the funeral home. He kissed my cheek which awoke me, and I was very frightened. But immediately I felt complete peace in my heart and have been able to accept this great loss ever since.

I just wanted to share these experiences with you and am so happy to do so.

The dreamer of these extraordinary and beautiful dreams went on to say that now she was not afraid of death and that she knew they would all join Gary in heaven someday. Then she wished God's blessing and sufficient strength for the family in this time of their sorrow.

That the friend's mother, rather than Gary's own mother, had these dreams seems strange. I cannot say why my sister did not have the comfort of such dreams. Perhaps she was comforted in a different way according to her unique need, or maybe she needed to receive her comfort through the dreams of another. (See this in the dreams of Don Bosco, chapter 9.)

The circumstances surrounding this death event were unusual. As Gary rode home from school, heavy rain had caused the car he was in to collide with another car. Gary had tried to protect another passenger by throwing himself over her when he saw they were going to be hit. This was not all. While at the hospital identifying the body, the family received a call that Randy, another son, was in a hospital in another part of town. At about the same time, he had been injured in a car accident on his way home from college classes.

When my sister called to tell me of Gary's death and to ask me to call members of our family, I was home from work, sick in bed with a respiratory infection. By the time I managed to complete the calls, I ached. I had such heaviness and constriction in my chest that I could hardly breathe. I thought this was due to the respiratory condition's being aggravated by my crying. Since then I have learned that physical pain of all kinds is an immediate and sometimes ongoing factor in grief.

After I made the calls, I had a kinesthetic hypnogogic dream. Fatigued and weak, I sank into a stage between wakefulness and sleep. I was comforted as I fell asleep. Then I felt myself being gathered up under huge, soft, fluffy wings that I thought of as God's. I remembered the Bible describing God as having wings. Later I found these two references:

> May you have a full reward from the LORD, the God of Israel, under whose wings you have come for refuge (Ruth 2:12).

> [O God]…hide me in the shadow of your wings (Ps 17:8).

Dreams May Focus on Other Issues

Sixteen years after her son, Gary, was killed in the car accident, my sister, Bea, had this dream.

> In the dream he's a happy little boy of about ten or eleven. He was being kept in jail although he hadn't done anything wrong. A man there was making him drink milk. I was feeling sorry for him because he was being mistreated, but he said, "It's all right, I can do it." I tell the man then that it is all right, that it's just that he's allergic to milk. Gary kept saying, "It's all right." He spoke in a gentle, reassuring manner, but "my heart is just broken, and I feel bad he's not being treated well."

Although Bea was deeply grieved in this dream, she did not think of it as a typical bereavement dream. The dream occurred many years after Gary's death and he appeared as a child instead of the young man he was when he died. Furthermore, she did not think of him as deceased. Instead, Bea thinks the dream refers to circumstances in her life in which something as nourishing as milk makes her as sick and as grief-stricken as when Gary's life was tragically taken. She felt imprisoned by certain circumstances and kept telling herself she could handle it.

Bea has always been thought of as a happy, fun-loving person. In school she was called Bubbles because she was always bubbling with pleasant laughter. When life went sour, she still maintained this image, always telling herself she could handle it.

This dream may express her pain for the loss of life as it might have been and as she wished it could have been.

Dreams That Occur Many Years after Death

Mama saw Helen in a dream; that was all she recalled. Mama did not say that her dream of her third daughter—who died fifty-seven years before—had comforted her in this tragic loss. However, it happened on Mother's Day. Her second daughter, Bea, had presented "A Tribute to Mother" at church, and someone had thoughtfully sent a cassette tape of it to Mama.

In this presentation the loss of her baby, Helen, was mentioned. What a lovely Mother's Day gift it was to receive a visit from a long-lost daughter along with gifts from her other children. I wonder if the dream may not have been giving Mama a glimpse of the not-too-distant future when she would be united with her baby; at the age of eighty-four, Mama knew she had already lived most of her life. I think many dreams about the deceased help to prepare us for our own death.

PART 2

Dreams Shared in Literature

Sharing what we read is a way of releasing possibilities to each other. I have come to believe that the artist within that created our dreams is reaching out to the artists beyond ourselves, the great writers, thinkers, engagers in life who can urge us through the pain into the mystery, the grandeur surrounding us. — Nan Zimmerman in *The Variety of Dream Experiences*

The dreams in this part are gleaned from my reading. They have been selected to fill in the gaps in my personal collection of dreams. Also, they further round out the variety of content in dream experiences about the deceased. For instance, I had no dreams of men about their wives who had died; so I have included dreams about wives from my reading. Men probably have as many dreams as women; but, being reserved about sharing their feelings, they do not share their dreams.

Dreams are feeling-oriented. They provide a safe way to acknowledge feelings and an outlet for tension. Writers and poets seem more inclined to share dreams, at least through writing. John Milton (1608-1674) is one of the best examples of a poet who gives expression in writing to the bereft feelings his dream evokes. His second wife had died at the age of thirty, four months after the birth of a child. In "Methought I Saw My Espoused Saint," Milton described her as she appeared to him in his dream and the disappointment of her fleeing as he awakened.

> ...vested all in white, pure as her mind.
> Her face was veiled, yet to my fancied sight
> Love, sweetness, goodness, in her person shines

So clear as in no face with more delight.
But O as to embrace me she inclined,
I waked, she fled, and day brought back my night.

A remarkable dream preserved a great epic poem. The dreamer, Jacapo, dreamed of his father, Dante, the great Italian poet and author of *Divine Comedy*, not long after his father's death. That is not so unusual. What is unusual is that Dante revealed to Jacapo where the ending for *Divine Comedy* was hidden.

Dante had worked on this epic, which consists of one hundred cantos, for many years. It is an account of his pilgrimage through the afterlife, according to the medieval understanding, in which his beloved wife, Beatrice, who had preceded him in death, becomes his guide when he reaches Paradise.

Dante had hidden the last thirteen cantos, and they were not found until his son dreamed about them. As a result, we find that Dante ended his pilgrimage when he reached the presence of God and his angels (Boorstin 263).

Other dreams in this part of the book illustrate the universal nature of dreams throughout history and in all nationalities. I have also included dreams about deceased friends.

5. Dreams about Deceased Parents and Grandparents

This section contains dreams about deceased parents and grandparents, which I have gleaned from literature. My research has shown that these dreams occur across cultures and religions and history. I have included examples from Africa, Japan, and Switzerland as well as from the seventeenth century.

Sometimes the Deceased Do Not Appear in Dreams

Some bereavement dreams do not include an appearance by the deceased loved one, but they can be comforting as well. Professor James Gollnick, of the University of Toronto, relates such a dream in his book *Dreams in the Psychology of Religion.*

This dream occurred five days after his mother's unexpected death. He describes himself as numb with shock and grief as he traveled to the funeral and as he sorted her papers, pictures, and other things.

> I am walking at night in a thick fog. I can only see a few steps in front of me. Suddenly, I notice something bright straight ahead and above me. I am struck by the beauty and strange quality of the light as it approaches. It

appears to be a cross in a circle—both are on fire. I walk in that direction and feel fortunate to have this beacon to orient me in the darkness (127).

Gollnick says that when he awoke from this dream, he felt as if he had received a mysterious and extraordinary gift. The brilliance of the circled cross was a sign of divine presence when everything around him seemed shrouded in fog.

Over a year after my mother's death, I had a strange dream that left me feeling sad. I felt it was related to my mother's death, although she did not appear in it. In fact the main characters were two trees, which are not shown in the dream. I call it my Fallen Tree Dream.

> I am looking over the damage done by a storm. Another woman is with me. A tree has blown down. I think of it as being in the yard of my childhood home, although I don't see a house. The sun is shining and wet plants and grass glisten. Everything is beautiful and fresh. A man appears and pulls a brown tree limb away. He says the town council won't be able to meet under the trees now. I explain to the woman that there used to be two large trees. I feel sad about losing the trees, saying I will miss them, but it looks nice anyway. Maybe we can do without them.

The time of my dreaming was a couple of weeks after my brothers, my sister, and I had met at our family home for a few days; it was the first time we'd seen one another since our mother's death. I hadn't connected this to the dream until I shared it with Gayle Delaney, a dream consultant and friend. She reminded me of the time factor by asking if the dream was around the time of my mother's birthday. It wasn't, but the family gathering came to mind. After that revelation, I could understand the images.

The storm represents my mother's death and her lengthy, painful illness. The tree that had blown down in the dream was an old walnut tree that had grown in our yard. It was diseased and had finally died after being struck by lightning several times.

Not only does the tree in my dream represent the old walnut tree, but it represents Mama when disease struck her down after a long time. The second tree was an apple tree, which represents my father who had been dead eight and one-half years. A porch swing had hung from the branches of these trees and connected them. As children, we used to play under these trees and in the swing.

Here we had rested in the shade and had played on summer evenings after the farm work was done; here uncles had discussed events and family interests with our father and grandfather. Now the trees and people (the town council) are gone— taken by the storms and transitions of life. I believe this dream is not only mourning my mother but my father and my past as well. Although I wouldn't refer to my past as "the good old days," it is part of who I am. The dream does not show the storm, the trees, nor the people. Instead, it shows a sunny day with fresh foliage glistening with raindrops. In other words, I am moving on with my living without the people and trees of my childhood, but I am not forgetting them. There is a sense of peace after the storm.

A Seventeenth-Century Japanese Poet's Dream

Kikaku, a seventeenth-century Japanese poet, was awakened by the cuckoo bird while dreaming of his dead mother. He chided the bird for interrupting his dream and causing her to leave. This poem is translated from the Japanese in two different ways in my two haiku books. Either way, it expresses that the dream was comforting to the dreamer.

> In dreams she arrives.
> My mother. Why send her back?
> O heartless cuckoo.
> (*One Hundred Famous Haikus* 75).

> Cuckoo, did you cry
> To frighten away
> My mother
> Watching in my dream?
> (*Haiku Harvest* 17).

A Mother's Love

Sophy Burham recalls three visits from her mother after her death, but she does not say how these visits occurred. Since she does not mention that they were dreams and she uses the word *phantom,* the visits probably came about through visions or hypnogogic dreams. Hypnogogic dreams are those images that come to us when we are not fully awake or completely asleep.

> Her last visit was the most dramatic. I was lying in the pretty little canopy bed in "my" room, my childhood room, the room—the very bed—she had died in. It was 10 or 11 at night. I was reading. The light was on. [This may indicate she was in that time between being awake and being asleep that occurs when a person falls asleep while reading.]
>
> Suddenly my mother was standing in the doorway. I looked up, saw her, and—I burst into tears. *How can I live without my mother?* I thought.
>
> It was not her presence in the doorway that upset me, or that she had come to fulfill her pledge and tell me about The Other Side. It was that she stood there smiling at me with such unbearable love. She stood there, a phantom without any of the barriers that had always separated us—barriers of culture and of our different memories, barriers of anger and judgmentalness, or any of the petty hurts we had inflicted on each other. This was the pure essence of my mother, looking at me with such love I thought my heart would break.
>
> *How can I live without my mother?* I thought. She took a step backward in concern: She hadn't meant to hurt me....

I suddenly understood, we are not *supposed* to meet so totally. We are not strong enough to take such undiluted love.

> Concerned, apologetic, she faded away. I have not seen her since...[ten years later], [I would like to]....This time

maybe I'd remember to ask about death and life. But I believe that possibly we are not supposed to know (13-15).

Recurring Coffin Dreams

Susan Zulu, a Zambian woman,[1] came to Nelson Hayashida, who was a missionary teaching in Zambia at the time, for help with troubling dreams that began after her mother's death. Susan was thirty-eight, married, and a second-generation Christian. After her mother died, Susan dreamed that her mother came to her on the same night. From that time (1983) until telling this to Hayashida (about five years later), she had dreamed of people carrying the coffin of a dead body. Susan gave a summary of her dreams, which follows in her own words:

> This is my mother who died some time ago....Mainly I dream about this dead body being carried and thereafter I see the mother appearing, although I see white men with Bibles but they disappear and the same dead body and my mother appear again. After those people have come and even given me a Bible, all of a sudden they disappear and these bad dreams come again.
> [I understand her to be saying she had dreams of the dead body, then she had a dream in which white men with Bibles come and give her a Bible and disappear. After that she had more dreams in which her mother appears in the coffin.] I sometimes talk to my mother [in dreams], but when I wake up, I forget what we were talking about.[2]

---

1 In telling the other dreams in this book, I have not indicated the race or nationality of the dreamer, but in this story, it seems to be of some significance in understanding the dream.

2 This account of Susan's story was first published in Hayashida's article, "Dreams: A Way of Revelation for the African Church." He also includes it in his dissertation, "Significance of Dreams" (233-35), which is the first treatment of African Christian dreams and visions on a systematic scale using data collected from a particular mission church, the Baptists of Zambia.

When Hayashida asked Susan how she felt when she saw the coffin and her mother, she replied as follows:

> When I see the coffin, I was ffearing. Sometimes, but since it has been happening for a long time, I'm now used to it. When I see my mother, she even sits up and we start discussing. When my mother comes with an anger, I try to fly to get away, but my mother follows and tries to grab me back. One time she grabbed me. After grabbing me, I feel weak and some pain. Up to now I'm still troubled and I think as to why the dead mother should come to me in a dream always.

Susan said she had told her family about these dreams. She also went to traditional African doctors, who said the dream came from demons and gave her medicines, which did not help. She did not tell the members of her church anything about her dreams.

Hayashida asked Susan about the white men with Bibles. She said she had dreamed of them when her mother was still living and they both were going to church together. She stopped going to church when her mother died.

Hayashida wisely told her that he could not interpret her dreams. He gently counseled her to ask God to give her understanding and to come to her own conclusions.

Susan's confusion regarding the difference between cultures and religions may have prolonged her grieving and contributed to her recurring dreams. Traditionally, Africans value dreams and tend to live out of their understanding of them. With its emphasis on outer realities and science, Western culture tends to ignore dreams. They are even devalued as out-of-date and superstitious. Thus, Africans today may be ambivalent about the place of dreams. They continue to dream—as we all do, since we are created that way—but today's prevailing culture does not give much value to dreams. "If dreams aren't important, then why do we dream?" Susan seems to be asking when she observes, "I think as to why the dead mother should come to me in a dream always."

Susan and her mother had accepted Christian beliefs. Mainline Christian churches seldom mention dreams and sometimes discredit them when they do, even though much of the Bible is composed of dreams and material related to dreams. Without the traditional rituals and beliefs in ancestral spirits that provided guidance for dreams, Susan may have been left without a way to express her grief.

In addition, a person's life is formed by her or his own culture and history. Such a person continues to be influenced by culture after conversion takes place (Hayashida).

I am writing from a non-African viewpoint and I have not had the opportunity to check this out with the dreamer. But I find the following features of the bereavement dream in Susan's dreams:

- **The disturbing appearance of the deceased person.** These painful experiences of seeing her mother as a corpse in a coffin help the dreamer get used to the reality of the death. Through these recurring dreams, Susan begins to think of her mother as no longer living and makes some adjustment to ongoing life. Dreams in which the dead appear in the coffin are common in all cultures. I see them reported in almost everything I read on the subject. Although such dreams suggest the idea of resurrection in which the dead rise from the coffin, they also have a personal meaning.

- **Comforting experiences.** Usually these experiences are pleasant appearances of the deceased; in Susan's dream, however, comfort was offered through the gift of the Bible, which contains comforting messages. Unfortunately, she did not recognize this and was not comforted.

- **Conversation with the deceased.** Sometimes the loved one appears in a dream with reassuring words, but if mourning has gone on too long, the deceased may scold the dreamer. In Susan's dream her mother may be telling her it is time to stop grieving by grabbing her back. This would be a physical way of saying, "Come back here. Face it. I'm dead." Susan might benefit from being asked to think about what her mother is grabbing her back to. This might lead her to see that she is being brought back to face the reality of the death from which she is fleeing. There may be an additional meaning, which I will discuss a little later in this section.

- **Unresolved feelings of guilt, self-reproach, and anger.** The bereaved often feel guilty when they do not live up to parental expectations. They break away to live their own individual lifestyles. Susan had stopped going to "worship" after her mother died. She may have felt guilty at dishonoring her mother in this way.

- **Religious images.** The church, preachers, and Bibles are associated with her mother. This may indicate that Susan is struggling on a subconscious level with whether to allow herself to be pulled back to church and worship. I see this in the way the dream shows her the religious figures and then shows her mother, which she associates with them, grabbing her back. Susan should come to these conclusions herself. However, giving her questions to ponder might help break her negative, fearful mind-set.

My experiences with dream work lead me to believe that by accepting her dreams as natural to the mourning process and by seeing the positive influences in them, Susan's "bad" dreams would cease.[3]

---

3 An additional theme that I find suggested by Susan's dreams is the encounter with death itself as a condition of life. Susan's mother may literally be representing herself in the grieving aspect of her dreams, and she may also represent death. Acceptance of death as a condition of life must come from

Coffin dreams are not unusual and other accounts appear in this book. In *The Dreams of Women*, Lucy Goodison, a British writer, tells of a British woman's recurring dream of her dead mother rising from the coffin (152-55).

The mother had required her children to be perfect and had used her illness to control them. Of course, this resulted in much anger; thus, when the mother died, the dreamer felt only relief. Dreams in which the mother rose to a sitting position in the coffin caused the dreamer to feel that she was still bound to her dominant mother.

A friend suggested that she talk to the person who kept appearing this way in her dreams. The dreamer took her friend's advice and told her mother, "You're dead and I'm alive. You're where you are and can get on with that." Then she declared the same about herself. After confronting her mother about the coffin, she challenged her to let go and forget and indicated she was willing to do the same. Worked with in this way, the dream became the basis for moving beyond the conflict with the mother, and the coffin dreams ended.

Receiving Help from the Deceased

Joyce Muyamba was thirty, married with five children, and a Christian for four years at the time she told this dream.

> Once (one month ago) I dreamed of my mother who
> passed away. When she came to me, I tried to follow her.
> When I followed, she fell down. I found she was dead
> when I got there. By then I was crying and my husband
> woke me up.

This was a perplexing dream for Joyce. It sounds like a grief dream that helps the bereaved accept what is known—that the mother really is dead (Hayashida, "Significance of Dreams," 230).

---

within on a deep feeling level and usually develops gradually. Dreams can be very useful in helping this acceptance to develop.

Planning a Funeral Many Years after the Death

Wayne Oates, professor of Psychiatry and Behavior Science at the University of Louisville School of Medicine, shared this dream of his grandmother many years after her death. On the day of the dream he had taken a tour of Forest Lawn Cemetery near Glendale, California, where he had been for some lectures. He was bothered by the display of "sentimental religion, ardent patriotism, and near worship of the dead," as well as by the large sum of money and real estate involved when there were so many needy people. He found himself remembering his own background of poverty and the grandmother who had cared for him.

> That night I dreamed about my grandmother long
> deceased. She had been the beloved person who cared
> for me as an infant and child while my mother worked.
> Now in my dream we were having her funeral all over
> again. I dreamed that I personally had arranged it all, a
> $10,000 funeral, including a real Irish wake! Everyone
> had a great time—even my grandmother, who was dead,
> and yet not dead. It was her funeral we were having, but
> she too was there to enjoy the festivities, all the beauty,
> all the luxury that I had provided! (45).

Obviously, this dream was connected with the previous day's experience at the plush Forest Lawn Cemetery. When his grandmother died during the Great Depression, they had hardly had enough money to bury her in the least expensive way. He even recalled conflict over who would pay for the funeral. "Now," he says, "it was as if the dream was an undoing of all this privation, an attempt at overdoing the funeral" (45).

That he would dream a classic wish-fulfillment dream about his grandmother after so many years amazed him.

A Double Loss

Ellen, a nurse, dreamed of her grandfather six months after his death. In her dream she was a nurse in the hospital where her grandfather was hospitalized. She was involved with the technical procedures of caring for him. She was telling him not to move and not to massage his legs because this could dislodge a clot and cause another heart attack. Then the scene shifted, and she saw "huge cartons of Campbell's soup and these were being sent to different countries like South America. I awoke sobbing and crying" (Ullman and Zimmerman 146-47).

Ellen had been close to her grandfather. Following his death, a number of projects were initiated in memory of the many good deeds he had performed. This explains the reference to huge cartons of soup for the needy.

Ellen associated the warning in the dream regarding his legs to the loss of her leg, which had been replaced with a prosthesis. Her dream appears to be a response to a double loss. Skilled technical help had not prevented the death of her grandfather or the loss of her leg, both permanent losses. While the dream content itself is not directly comforting, it does provide a release for Ellen and this is healing. It is not unusual to grieve for a previous loss along with a new loss.

Happy Memories about Grandfather

Vicente Aleixandre begins his poem "My Grandfather's Death" by telling about hearing the painful breathing of his sick grandfather and the sounds of people entering and leaving the house as he went to sleep. The poem continues with the young child dreaming that he and his grandfather were out in a boat catching big fish. The sea is smooth and beautiful. A fresh breeze in the sunlight did not disturb the sea. His grandfather's face was kind as usual, and with his hand he pointed out the sparkles and crests on the water and the hazy, happy coastline. The boy felt so happy to be alone with his grandfather, so big and secure out on the sea. He didn't want to reach their destination too soon. His white-haired, blue-eyed grandfather laughed and started to tell a story. With the rocking boat being pushed along by his grandfather's voice, the boy went to sleep (a dream within a dream). Suddenly the boat stopped as if it had struck something, and he awakened to silence.

Although reality asserts itself and the poet awakens to the truth, I feel as if this was a comforting dream that gave him a happy memory and helped dim the painful picture of his grandfather's dying.

Asking the Deceased to Visit in the Daytime

Phil George, a Native American whose tribal name is Two Swans Ascending from Still Waters, had so many visits from his grandmother in his dreams that he tried burning sage, keeping a spruce bough by his bed, and sprinkling tobacco on water to keep the nightmares away. He was in Vietnam when she died and could not return home. The frequent dream visits may have helped him make the loss real. Finally, he asks her in his poem "The Visit":

> Grandmother, let's visit—
> Talk and laugh when
> Sun is shining;
> So I may sleep, rest at night.

A Swiss Psychologist Dreams of Her Father

Marie-Louise von Franz was away from home when her father died suddenly. She describes herself as relatively young at the time. This is her first dream three weeks after his death.

> It was about ten o'clock in the evening, dark outside. I heard the doorbell ring and "knew" at once somehow that this was my father coming. I opened the door and there he stood with a suitcase. I remembered from the *Tibetan Book of the Dead* that people who died suddenly should be told that they are dead, but before I could say so he smiled at me and said: "Of course I know that I am dead, but may I not visit you?" I said: "Of course, come in," and then asked, "How are you now? What are you doing? Are you happy?" He answered: "Let me remember what you, the living, call happy. Yes, in your language, I am happy. I am in Vienna (his hometown which he

loved and longed for all his life) and I am studying at the
music academy." Then he went into the house, we
climbed the stairs and I wanted to lead him to his former
bedroom. But he said: "Oh, no, now I am only a guest,"
and went up to the guestroom. There he put his suitcase
down and said: "It is not good for either the dead or the
living to be together too long. Leave me now. Good
night." And with a gesture he signalled me not to
embrace him, but to go. I went into my own room,
thinking that I had forgotten to put out the electric stove
and that there was a danger of fire. At that moment I
woke up, feeling terribly hot and sweating (111-12).

This dream came naturally at a time the dreamer was preoccupied with her father's unexpected departure. How comforting
it must have been to have her father drop in for a visit in her
dream, and to learn that he is happy pursuing something he
loved and always wanted to do. When he says he comes only
as a guest, the dream reinforces his being gone from our
time-space existence. He tells her in no uncertain terms that he
is dead.

In addition to being comforting, the appearance of the dead
loved one repeating the information known to the dreamer—that
he or she is dead—aids the dreamer in assimilating the reality.
This is what I see in this dream.

Dr. von Franz thinks waking up "terribly hot" might be a strong
physical counterreaction as a healing defense against the chill of
death. As a psychologist, von Franz was doing research on the
dreams of the dying at this time. The "danger of fire" appears to
mean that the death of her father was getting too close to her
own life to be comfortable.

In this dream of her father, and in similar dreams of others,
von Franz sees that "something gets lost at death....Much of what
one calls 'human warmth' seems to disappear." In the deceased
loved one, "wishing, fearing and desiring of the ego seems to
cease." Von Franz says that this is sometimes observed with dying
people whose reactions are strangely "far away" and "detached,"
as if human relations no longer matter (111). About six weeks

after her father's death, von Franz had a second dream in which he appeared healthy and alive. But she said she knew in the dream that he was dead. He spoke to her in cheerful excitement, saying, "the resurrection of the flesh is a reality. Come with me, I can show it to you." He took her to the cemetery and pointed to a grave and called out, "Here, for instance, come and look." She saw the earth begin to move and stared in that direction, full of dread that a half-decomposed corpse was about to appear. Then she saw that a shining golden-green crucifix was drilling its way upward out of the earth. Her father called out, "Look here! *This* is the resurrection of the flesh" (133).

Von Franz associated the expression "resurrected in Christ" with the dream as a whole. The *animated* crucifix of green-gold metal suggested alchemy to her. In the Middle Ages, alchemists tried to change base metals into gold and to make a compound that would cure all disease and extend life indefinitely. Therefore, it was a way of expressing everlasting life. Still von Franz says of the dream, "It is a mystery that one cannot fathom" (133). Continuity of life is the message of this dream.

The following account is of von Franz's dream of her father five years after his death:

> I was with my sister and we both wanted to take Tram No. 8 at a certain place in Zurich, to go to the center of town. We leaped onto the tram and discovered too late that it was going in the opposite direction. I said to my sister, "If one of us had done this it would be just a mistake, but since both of us have done it, then there must be a meaning in it. Let's watch out for what it may lead to." Then there came a so-called "controlleur," who checked the tickets. On his cap were the letters "EWZ," which stands for Electricity Works of Zurich. I wondered why such a man would be the controlleur. At the next tram stop we got off and there a taxi drove up near us and out of it—came my father! I knew it was his ghost. When I started to greet him, he made a sign not to come too near him and then walked away to the house where he lived. I called after him, "We don't live there any

more." But he shook his head and murmured, "That doesn't matter to me now" (149).

Von Franz understood this whole dream to be a symbolic statement about another reality. It came to her in the context of her work investigating how dreams consciously prepare us for the end of this life and for a continuation of the life process in a transformed state after death. She seemed to understand this dream and perhaps her other dreams to be more concerned with this issue than with grief.

Traditional methods of working with images and symbols are not very productive for figuring out the meaning of the dream. Nevertheless, von Franz makes some associations with important motifs. To her, *No. 8* represents timelessness, eternity, and completeness. *Controlleur* reminds her of the control used in seances by spiritualists as a connection between the medium and the *spirit*. This strange controlleur did bring the dreamer in touch with her father's ghost; however, since the workman was from the Electric Works, a flow of energy seems to be involved. Von Franz thinks that he may represent a control that goes on between time and space existence and existence without time and space, which explains after-death appearances in dream and visionary experiences. The dream definitely makes it clear that her father is not confined to a physical place and a physical body by saying that it doesn't matter that her father does not live in their house any more.

While von Franz does not say whether this dream helped her in the grief process, there is a suggestion that the dream was reporting to her that she was accepting her father's death.

There is a pattern of meeting-parting, meeting-parting in von Franz's dreams that is typical of many bereavement dreams. There is no indication that the parting is difficult. There is more of a feeling of wonder that these meetings take place at all.

Recurrent Dreams

Ann Landers's column carried a letter from a reader about a recurring dream he had of his father fifteen years after his death

("Anybody Else 'Haunted by Their Father?'"). In this dream, the deceased father shows up at the front door of the dreamer's home. He is hiding out and leading a totally different life, and the dreamer is the only one who knows this. He pleads with his father to admit that he really isn't dead, but the father refuses and leaves. Others in the dream accept his reappearance and departure.

The dreamer wonders why he does not ask his father about the so-called afterlife. I will play Ann Landers here and give a response. The dream is to encourage him to let go of his father so he can get on with his own life. The father refuses to admit he is not dead because he is dead. Of course, he can reappear and depart in memories and dreams. He does live in a different dimension, not in flesh and blood, so it could be said that he is hiding (he cannot be seen).

I think the dream is trying to tell the dreamer in every way possible that everyone else accepts his father's death, so he needs to be more concerned with life and less with the afterlife. Being willing to let go is part of living.

Nevertheless, I sympathize with this dreamer. It is beyond belief for someone we love or know to stop existing in time and space as a flesh-and-blood presence. How can a person as significant in our lives as a father just stop being?

6. Dreams about Deceased Spouses

The literature shows that bereavement dreams are common to many cultures and periods of history. The sampling I present here ranges from a modern-day psychologist's dreams about her husband to a fourth-century Chinese man's dreams about his wife to a seventh-century Japanese court lady's dreams about her emperor to the dreams of nineteenth-century Zulu women. These dreams help the dreamers accept the reality of their loved ones' death and provide comfort and healing. The dreamer may also experience physical sensations, especially if the death was traumatic.

A Healing Dream

In her book *Something More,* Catherine Marshall tells of the dream experiences of a writer she met at the first *Guideposts* writers' workshop. The writer's wife had died following a lingering two-year illness. She had been left totally paralyzed, but with a sharp mind. He had cared for her forty hours a week as well as for their four children, their home, and his job. Six years later and after remarriage, he was still tormented by a recurring dream. This is the way he told his dream; notice the searching behavior in it.

> I am hurrying to the hospital. When I get there I cannot
> find Babs's room. Frantically, I go from floor to floor,
> room to room, calling her name. My panic and frustration
> grow by the minute because I know how much she
> needs me.
> Finally, I stumble into the right room. There she is as
> always, unable to move, sobbing my name.
> Then I awaken in a cold sweat, tears on my face. The
> nightmare has drained so much emotional energy I can
> hardly get out of bed and go to work (Marshall 97-8).

Marshall, who was also a participant at the workshop, says he
did not tell anyone of his nightmare problems. The others who
cared for him in this relaxed, creative setting sensed his need.

When he returned home, his wife observed a new calmness
in him. A few nights later he dreamed this last dream.

> As so often before, I am hurrying to the hospital.
> (Strange! I always know I am dreaming, but can do
> nothing about it.) *Oh God! Not again—please. Don't let it
> begin all over again.*
> But this time when I reach the hospital there is nothing
> of the usual frantic searching. I go directly to Babs's
> room. She smiles up from the bed and oh, joy! extends
> her arms to me! She is no longer paralyzed!
> She takes my face in her hands and calls my name and
> great waves of joy, unimaginable joy, rise up in me.
> She asks me to put her in the wheelchair as I'd done so
> often before. I start pushing her toward the elevator to
> the roof thinking she'd like to soak up some sunshine,
> but she says, "No, not the roof. Take me in there"
> (Marshall 99).

Attending a workshop indicates the grieving husband's willingness to move on with his life and to be open to the caring of
others. His prayer in his dream that it be over also expressed his
willingness on a deep level to be through with the agony of such
a long period of grieving. His dream reviewed pleasant memo-

ries, reassured him of Babs's well being, and provided a spiritual blessing as it continued as follows:

> I turn in the direction she is pointing and find a room full of people. It's the library at the retreat house on the Sound where my little Workshop group met.
>
> As I wheel Babs into the room, the people come to greet her. Great rays of light, love-light, radiate from her as she holds out her hands to each of them!
>
> My happiness is beyond belief. There are tears of happiness in my eyes. Yet, there's much more joy to come.... When Babs has greeted each Workshopper, she says, "I want to stand." And suddenly she's on her feet!
>
> Then the scene shifts to Oakland, where Babs was born. We're walking beside Lake Merritt as we used to long ago. She's laughing and twirling like a girl full of life and happiness. Then she puts her head caressingly on my shoulder—and the dream ends.
>
> When I awoke, I bolted straight upright in bed. My usually heavy heart felt feather-light, gay. There was the unmistakable feeling of having been in God's presence. The messages of the dream were so plain: Babs was no longer paralyzed and was extremely happy.
>
> God had let me know that He loves me. There is an assurance—a knowing—that I'll never have the nightmare again (Marshall 100).[1]

This dreamer has never had another nightmare. In her book Marshall said that she felt that God's spirit had used this workshop to bring deep emotional and psychic healing to this terribly wounded and grieved person, and this final dream confirmed it.

---

1 Something to note in this dream is that this time, when he is aware that he is dreaming, he prays for help. This demonstrates a dream situation in which there is cooperation between the conscious waking state and the subconscious dream state. Bringing the conscious and subconscious together into a harmonious relationship may be one way our dreams can help us in bereavement.

Physical Sensations
in Dreams Accompanying Traumatic Deaths

Edmund Wilson records in his private journals a series of dreams about his second wife, Margaret, after her accidental death in 1932. These dreams continued through 1940. The editor of the published volumes says, "The dreams suggest profound and unresolved feelings, continuing grief and self-blame" (367).

Wilson awoke from some of his dreams with convulsive twitching. Physical sensations can be quite strong in dreams. I have noticed this in dreams in which death has occurred in connection with a severe trauma. I tell about one such dream experience in my previous book about dreams, *Discovering My Biblical Dream Heritage.* When the dreamer awoke from a dream about his murdered parents, he felt as though his whole body was in a painful spasm. Despite this, the dream comforted him through his father's telling him "not to worry, that everything was all right." Usually the feeling of the dream in the body is not so strong. The dreamer may not even be aware of it.

Wilson's dreams also suggest strong feelings—guilt for not being able to help Margaret and disappointment that he would never see her again. His sense of abandonment, her appearance and disappearance, and the searching are typical of grief dreams. This intense grieving might appear lengthy to the point of being pathological, going on as it did for five or six years according to his journal. However, some studies challenge the belief that mourners should recover from a loss within a set time. The circumstances and cause of death can make a difference in the emotional course taken by the grieving. Margaret's death was due to an accidental fall. A study of spouses and parents of auto accident victims found that they were grieving more and were more depressed, hostile, and worried four to seven years after the loss than a comparable group who had not had such a loss.

A Romantic Walk

Lines from Antonio Machado's (1875-1939) untitled poem to his dead wife, Leonor, tell of his dream of being with her.

I dreamed you led me
along a white footpath
through green fields
toward the blue mountain
one serene morning.

I felt your hand in mine,
your companion hand,
your child voice in my ear
like a new bell,
the pristine bell
of a spring dawn.
It was your voice and hand....

Dreams of a Fourth-Century Chinese Wife

P' An Yueh, a fourth-century Chinese, writes in "In Mourning for His Dead Wife" of seeing her alive in his dreams. He longs for his wife to listen to his secrets. He feels he has no reason to live and just goes through the motions of doing his job at court. When he goes home, he expects to see her. He thinks he sees her shadow on the screens and curtains. He describes her letters as the most precious examples of calligraphy and is haunted by her perfume. Her clothes still hang in the closets. She vanishes when he awakens, leaving him in sorrow. The wife's vanishing after a visit in a dream may be the dream's way of helping the husband get used to his loss.

A Surgeon's Wife Expects and Gets Dreams

Anne M. Brooks recorded her personal grief in a once-a-month journal for the year following her surgeon husband's death of cancer at age sixty-four. This journal is published in a book entitled *The Grieving Time*. This nonclinical, spontaneous, emotional account of struggling with personal grief is comforting and healing to those who read it.

Apparently Brooks expected dreams as she asks herself in the second month of grief, "Why can't I dream of him?" She laments, "I simply cannot visualize his face or form." In the third month she exclaims, "I am finally dreaming of him! It is such a comfort, so natural. At first he was only a shadowy figure, a presence but now he is there!" In the tenth month she has what she calls a "real" dream and wakes up truly happy for the first time in a year.

In this dream she is sitting with her husband on a beach. He looks healthy and tan and is smiling as he tells her he isn't going to take any more courses in anything because he knows all he wants to know. She could feel the warmth of his hand when she held it.

To expect dreams is a good way to encourage dreaming. I do want to suggest that if dreams are not recalled, the bereaved person should not be alarmed or take it as a deprivation. It may be that some persons are comforted in other ways and dreams are not necessary or even the best way for the grieving to be comforted.

A Miracle Dream

Joyce Brothers shares her dreams and the part they played in her overwhelming grief when her husband of forty-two years died. As a psychologist, she knew all the reactions she would probably experience, but she was not prepared for their intensity. She says that she did not manage grief better than any other widow.

Her husband, Milt, had cancer; he was in pain and nothing pleased him. In her first dreams he appeared as he was in the last eighteen months of his life and he was always angry with her. Just the same she was happy that he was there. The dreams were so real that she felt lonelier than ever when she awoke. Actually, these dreams appear to be a review of the end of his life and the end of her life with him as she had known and enjoyed it.

Then the second spring after Milt died, she had what she called the Miracle Dream. It came after she had a one-sided conversation with him on the anniversary of his funeral. She described this dream as the beginning of a number of long steps forward.

In this dream she says the two of them were at their farm in a hard snow with a fire on the hearth. The house was warm with the smell of the gingerbread she had just baked. The scene changed to the outdoors. The snowing had stopped, and the sun was out bright. She and her husband were slipping and sliding on the snow on the way down the hill toward the brook. They were holding hands and laughing. Daffodils were blooming on low, woody bushes and gave the impression of a fantasy land. They picked some flowers the dinner table. On the way back home, she told her husband how lovely it was to have a second chance to be with him. The feeling of pleasure and closeness stayed with her even after waking.

Even the dreams with unpleasant content were comforting to her because they alleviated her loneliness. Others have told me that this was their experience, too.

I suspect Dr. Brothers responded to the total impact of her Miracle Dream, but I think the lovely imagery invites even the reader or listener to linger over it. The setting is at their farm, a place they both loved. Seasonal imagery is used within the dream in the way we often describe cycles of grief in waking life: Winter snow gives way to spring flowers, depicting moving from the coldness and stillness of death in early grief to the warmth and renewal of life in resolving grief. Besides these outer symbols of change, marvelous imagery depicts warmth and life within: a warm fire in the fireplace, spicy gingerbread from the oven, and laughter in the bright sunlight. The fragrance of the gingerbread enhances the pleasure of the occasion. Taste and smell very seldom occur in dreams. This is a special dream indeed. And arms full of flowers denote the abundant life. Fantasy land lets her know that this is not the way of waking life, but it suggests that through memories she can be with her husband. The bad memories of the end are giving way to the good memories of former times.

A Dream Poem

A Japanese court lady who lived in the seventh century records in poetry her dream of Emperor Tenji. Translated by Geoffrey

Bownas and Anthony Thwaite, the poem says she saw her Lord in the night in her sleep. In the morning she longs for him and wishes he were a jade bracelet she could wear on her arm or a robe she could put on and never take off.

Feelings of Guilt over Enjoying Life

The following lines are from a poem by Olga Berggolts, a Russian woman. Her first husband was executed during Stalin's purges of the thirties. Her second husband died of hunger during the German blockade of Leningrad in 1942. Olga dreamed of her second husband coming to her even after she was remarried and living in a different house. Her poem describes "the persistence of loyalty in the unconscious, even when the survivor has entered a new relationship."

> I saw you—you were alive...
> You were earth already, ashes,...
>
> You passed through war hell, concentration camp,
> through furnace...
> through your own death you...
> came out of love for me....
>
> You found my house, but I live now
> not in our house, in another;
> and a new husband shares my waking hours...
> O how could you not have known!
>
> Like the master of the house, proudly you crossed
> the threshold, stood there lovingly....
>
> O my friend, forgive me....

The Dreams of Nineteenth-Century Zulu Women

An 1865 publication tells of Zulu women seeing their deceased husbands as if they were still living and complaining:

> I am troubled by the father of So-and-so: he does not
> leave me; it is as though he was not dead; at night I am

always with him, and he vanishes when I am awake. At
length my bodily health is deranged; he speaks about his
children, and his property, and about many little matters
(Callaway 316).

To bar such dreams, these women followed a ritual with
medicine prescribed by their doctors.

Dreamer's Husband Comes
to Family Christmas Celebration

Meaningful dreams often come to us at special times. Two of
my own dreams are reported later in this book—Circle of Grief
(chapter 13) on my birthday and You've Done a Good Job
(chapter 10) on Mother's Day. Two other special dreams shared
in *Discovering My Biblical Dream Heritage* are My Sister's
Christmas Gift (157) and Looking into the Pool (165), which I
dreamed on my thirty-third wedding anniversary. My mother also
had a special Mother's Day dream at age eighty-four, which I
discussed in chapter 4. These are not part of mourning a loved
one, but they do illustrate that dreams deal with a variety of issues
at such times, and grief can be one of them.

Holidays and family celebrations often bring comforting
dreams about the deceased loved one. Generally, these dreams
are pleasant and confirm that the dreamer has reached the stage
of coping with ongoing life in the grieving process. Evelyn's
dream of her daughter at Christmastime is one such dream
(chapter 4). Christmas seems to be our dream's favorite time for
comforting us in our bereavement. Here is a Christmas dream I
enjoyed reading.

> One Christmas morning I had a distinct dream or vision
> of Al standing at the door all dressed up and wearing
> something red, a scarf or a cumberbund [sic], and looking
> very handsome and a bit impish as if he were surprising
> us for Christmas. He gave me a warm kiss on the mouth
> and faded gently away....I got up full of good cheer
> determined to make the day a happy one and it was. As

we began our dinner with champagne, I told everyone of
my vision and we went happily on with the day...
(B. Siegel 255).

7. Dreams about Deceased Siblings

I read a pleasant dream in an article in *Pastoral Psychology* (Halligan and Shea) that provided the dreamer with reassurance regarding his sister. The dream also aided the dreamer in accepting death. The dreamer is trying to get to a school which had been renovated into a home for the elderly. When he realized the bus was not going where he needed to be, he got off. He asked the bus driver for directions, and the driver drew him a map and gave him written instructions. Then the scene changed and his older sister, who had died two years earlier, appeared and invited him to supper. She was no longer disabled and walked easily.

This is my understanding of the dream. The dreamer is trying to go to a place of learning (perhaps the school of life) that has been converted into a place where old people stay before they die. The way the dreamer was going (his attitude about death) was not right. Further directions were needed to help the dreamer reach the place that the elderly have reached, where they accept the end of life. The dream gives this direction by having the dreamer's deceased sister appear, happy and healthy, to invite him to partake of that which is as satisfying as food is to the living. In addition to dealing with his need to accept death, the dream provides comfort by presenting his sister who is in good health and who offers him comfort in the form of a meal.

8. Dreams about Deceased Children

Dreams of deceased children often bring comfort by allowing the parents to see that their child is all right and to be reassured that there is no more suffering. The inability to have children can also result in grief for what will never be and bereavement dreams.

An Expectant Father's Dreams

The child's age at the time of death is not a strong factor in the intensity of the grief reaction. Even the inability to bear children due to age or surgery, such as a hysterectomy, can result in grieving for the children that can never be. A miscarriage or a stillborn baby can be just as traumatic to some as the death of an infant or an older child (A. Siegel 169).

Alan Siegel tells how dreams brought healing to an expectant father whose wife's miscarriage after eight weeks of pregnancy nearly caused her death. Her recovery was slow and her ability to conceive again was doubtful. Her husband wondered why he felt numb and was not more upset about the miscarriage. His dreams showed him that he did have fear and sadness about the loss of the baby and his wife's condition, but in trying to be strong, he had unconsciously refused to acknowledge them.

One dream in particular helped him begin to recover. In it a woman was being helped to walk after she had recently had a baby. She had been a great soccer player before this happened, according to the dream. Now she had difficulty remembering what she was doing and complained of being very tired. To the dreamer the great soccer player represented his athletic wife who was a star player both at her job and as a caring wife. Seeing her appear weak for the first time had been upsetting, and he reacted with fear. This dream and others helped him realize that he had not accepted the loss and allowed him to appreciate that to have emotions is to be human (A. Siegel 255).

A Mother's Dream Helps Her Let Go

Morton Kelsey received a letter from a woman who told of dreaming about her son, Michael, soon after he was killed in a car accident. He appeared first in her dream as if he were in a picture that kept flashing and pulsating. He was seated on something low and was smiling. He was neat and clean, wearing a blue plaid cowboy shirt and corduroy pants.

Then he appeared in a second scene where she was washing dishes. This time he was wearing his red plaid flannel shirt and blue jeans and leaning against a pool table. She said, "Oh, Michael," and held out her arms. As she did so, he fell toward her saying, "Oh, Mom, someone cut off my breath." He disappeared before he fell into her arms and left her standing there.

Her son had looked so happy when he first saw her. Then his expression changed to sorrow, and he looked about to cry. She felt sad that she was not able to touch him. She awoke from the dream, calling to her husband that she had just seen Michael.

They discussed what he had been wearing. Her husband thought Mike had been wearing a yellow T-shirt when he left the house the day of the accident. However, when they looked through his clothes, they found the yellow T-shirt but the red flannel shirt was gone. Apparently Mike had changed shirts before he left. Why he appeared in a blue plaid cowboy shirt in the beginning of the dream is not discussed. Perhaps it implies that he is living in an after-death dimension.

What about the change in his expression and his saying his breath was being cut off? His mother thought the dream might be saying that if she held on to him, she would impede his soul's progress. She felt that God let her see her son one more time to reassure her that he was all right. This conclusion comforted her (Kelsey 123-24).

9. Dreams about Friends and Others

Dreams that follow the death of a loved one may focus on issues the dreamer needs to resolve before grieving can begin. Dreams can promote inner healing and the acceptance of past hurts. Don Bosco, an Italian priest who organized missionary activity on behalf of homeless boys, noted that dreams and visions were an important factor in directing his life and ministry. In actuality, visions are simply waking dreams that spontaneously and involuntarily intrude on periods of wakefulness instead of periods of sleep.

A Friend's Death Brings a Dream Promoting Family Peace

After the death of a loved one, dreams may deal with other matters that must be resolved before we can handle the present grief adequately. Actually the grief stirs up memories that our dreams insist that we spend time with both consciously and subconsciously. "Our memories provide an incredible tool for growth and development," writes Morton Kelsey in his book *Reaching: The Journey to Fulfillment,* by helping us understand the patterns that emerge in our lives (63).

The following is an example of a dream that helps the dreamer accept events in his life and promotes inner healing (Cliff 55-58): Two days after his friend, Winnie, died, a middle-aged Australian horse-trainer dreamed that he was back where he grew up. He and his family were cleaning up the family place for a celebration. Fine-looking Arabian horses appeared. He took a picture of an Australian Rugby League Football captain named Wally Lewis. Then there was the question of whether to perform a postmortem examination on Winnie.

This dream sounds like a hodgepodge of unrelated subjects that doesn't have much to do with mourning for Winnie, who does not even appear in the dream. But a little background information shows that this is not the case.

Winnie had died of cancer. The dreamer had a medical history of cancer. Two brothers had died of the disease, and he had undergone five major operations for skin cancer and feared its recurrence. His parents and a sister had died when he was young. The family that remained had abandoned him, saying God had taken their parents and sister because of his drinking. He had been sober for ten years and did not believe this accusation to be true. However, memories of the hurt and anger he had felt at being accused in this way surfaced with the loss of his friend.

These memories provided the background for the setting of the dream. It took him back to a time and place in his early years that was associated with unpleasantness. The dream celebration presented him with the way he wished things could have been in his family. But notice what he and his family are doing: they are cleaning up the family place. This image suggests cleaning up the destructive attitudes and feelings he has carried about his family.

This dream even suggests the resources the dreamer had for accomplishing his goal. Wally Lewis, a sports legend and a winner, was a positive image to keep before him. Winnie, unlike the critical members of his family, "had chosen an attitude toward suffering which gave the suffering meaning" (Cliff 57). She represented a faith that chooses God despite the outcome. The dream showed Winnie's and Wally's qualities as positive influences that the dreamer can emulate in his conscious life.

Fine-looking Arabian horses, an image of power, point to his skill and power as a horse-trainer; qualities that were available to him for his own help.

Then there was the question of the autopsy or postmortem examination, in which the body is examined to determine the cause of death. To me, the dream uses Winnie's death to introduce the idea of a postmortem of his inner life. Although he resisted the idea of an autopsy as mutilating in the dream, he did begin to study (dissect) the meaning of his dreams in waking life. He connected his refusal in the dream to the fear that he might need further surgery (mutilation). As it turned out, he did not need further surgery. Later dreams helped him understand and come to peace with past hurts, making inner healing possible.

An Anglican Priest Dreams of a Well-Known Writer

J. B. Phillips thinks that many people must experience the sense of nearness of those who have died. A parish priest and vicar in England, Phillips is known especially for *The New Testament in Modern English*. He writes about this unusual experience after the death of C. S. Lewis, the distinguished English author (1898-1962).

In recording his experiences, Phillips said he knew C. S. Lewis mostly through correspondence, having seen him only once. A few days after Lewis's death, Phillips was watching television when Lewis appeared in a chair a few feet away. He was in good health and happy. He spoke important words concerning difficult circumstances Phillips was experiencing. Afterward, it was interesting to Phillips that he had not been thinking about Lewis. A week later, Lewis appeared again. This time, Phillips was reading in bed when Lewis, again looking quite healthy, repeated the message of his first appearance. Phillips later mentioned his experiences to a retired bishop living in Dorset, England, who told him that this sort of thing happened all the time. Phillips observed that it never occurred to him to try to touch Lewis (Duncan 26-27).

It is puzzling when the dead seem to really appear. Because this usually happens when one is just falling asleep, I consider them hypnogogic dreams. Both times Phillips was in positions that invite sleep. Sophy Burham called these appearances "visits" (chapter 5). The important thing to know is that they are not an unusual part of the grieving process; people of all educational levels and all religious persuasions experience these "real" appearances. Most people do not readily share these experiences, perhaps because they do not know what to call them. I encourage you to call such an experience whatever is comfortable to you: "dream," "appearance," "visit," even "vision."

An Evangelist's Amusing Dream

Khadijeh, a woman born in 1880 to a Muslim family in a country in the Middle East, turned to the Christian faith after a long and difficult pilgrimage. She wrote several hymns of merit. At age seventy-seven she died in a Christian hospital. When she realized that she was going to die, she made arrangements for a Christian funeral and for her family to be notified after the funeral. This was done, and her family came for her body.

Khadijeh was buried as a Muslim after ritual cleansing in the hope that God might forgive her and have mercy on her soul. A disabled woman evangelist in the hospital had a dream several nights later in which Khadijeh came to her asking, "Why did you sing the first line of the hymn I wrote incorrectly? It doesn't make sense!" (Miller 104).

One of her hymns had been *sung* at the funeral, but the evangelist did not know then that the first line of the hymn actually had been changed in the hymnbook from Khadijeh's original version. The change was not great, but it had offended the author's poetic sense. This aspect of the dream is puzzling. Needless to say, the next edition of the hymnal used the original version.

Sometimes dreams of the most serious nature can be a bit amusing. I wonder if the evangelist and hospital workers might not have wondered about Khadijeh's devotion to the Christian faith when she arranged for her family to bury her as a Muslim.

The evangelist's dream could be a humorous, lighthearted way of reassuring her that Khadijeh remained a Christian believer.

A Nineteenth-Century Priest's Dream Series

Don Bosco (1815-1888) was an Italian priest who became famous for his devoted care of homeless boys. He organized an order for missionary activity, was canonized in 1934, and became known as St. John Bosco. Dreams were an important factor in directing his life and ministry. A beautiful dream in which Don Bosco's mother appeared after her death is included in the multi-volume *Biographical Memoirs of Saint John Bosco* (Lemoyne et al.):[1]

> In August 1860...he dreamed that he met her near the shrine of Our Lady of Consolation....She looked beautiful. "What? Are you really here?" Don Bosco asked. "Aren't you dead?"
>
> "I died, but I'm alive," Margaret replied.
>
> "Are you happy?"
>
> "Very happy." After several other questions, Don Bosco asked her if she had gone straight to heaven. Margaret answered negatively. He then inquired if several boys— whose names he mentioned—were in heaven, and he received an affirmative reply.
>
> "Now tell me," Don Bosco went on, "what is it that you enjoy in heaven?"
>
> "I cannot explain that to you."
>
> "Give me at least an idea of your happiness; let me see a glimmer of it!"
>
> Mamma Margaret then appeared radiant with majesty and clothed in a magnificent robe. As a large choir stood

---

1 "Pope Pius IX instructed Don Bosco to make a record of the way he had been inspired and directed by God through dreams" (Kelsey, Foreword, x). *The Biographical Memoirs of Saint John Bosco* is the most extensive record of religious dreams within Christian tradition. The only comparable record is that of Saint Gregory Nazianzen, who recorded by means of poetry God's use of dreams in directing his life.

in the background, she began to sing a song of love to God that was indescribably sweet and went straight to the heart, filling it and carrying it away with love. It sounded as if a thousand voices and a thousand tones—from the deepest bass to the highest soprano—had all been blended together masterfully, delicately, and harmoniously to form one single voice, notwithstanding the variety of tones and the pitch of the voices ranging from loud to the barely perceptible. Don Bosco was so enchanted by this most melodious singing that he thought he was out of his senses, and he was no longer able to tell or ask his mother anything. When Mamma Margaret had finished singing, she turned to him and said: "I'll be waiting for you…" (vol. 5, 375-7).

In this dream Mamma Margaret seems to be giving her son a glimpse of the joy he may expect in the life hereafter and preparing him for his own death.

In another dream she is comforting one of the boys who is ill. Then she announces the boy's death. The dream turns out to have been at the time the boy actually died.

Don Bosco had other dreams in which his mother appeared after her death. The following one seems to be a continuation of an early childhood dream, which was instrumental in his becoming an apostle to poor and neglected boys. In it his mother is assisting in directing his work with the boys. Although I have drastically condensed the dream, I think the essence of it is preserved.

Suddenly there was a knock at the door. I rose quickly and opened it. My mother—dead now for six years—was standing there. Breathlessly she gasped, "Come and see! Come and see!" What followed was an amazing episode with an enormous elephant, who represented an evil spirit, and Our Lady's statue, who actually turns into Our Lady. This sequence of the dream revealed information as to the spiritual condition and temptations of the boys of the Oratory. Mamma Margaret, my deceased mother, reappears and a banner is unfurled. It bore the

Inscription "Holy Mary, help Your forlorn children!" The boys marched behind it singing "Praise Mary, ye faithful tongues" (vol. 7, 213).

Don Bosco also experienced appearances of others in visions after their death. Visions are simply waking dreams in which images break into periods of wakefulness instead of periods of sleep. Just as with the dream, the images rise spontaneously, involuntarily, with as little conscious control; they are no different from those experienced in sleep.

Louis Colle, a pupil, died on April 3, 1881. Beginning with his death, he appeared many times to Don Bosco in both visions and dreams. The visionary appearances broke into wakefulness during the sharing of confessions, at Mass, during the preparation of sermons, in a corridor, and on a train journey. Don Bosco did not confuse either visionary or dream appearances with a physically alive person.

The day Louis died, Don Bosco was hearing confessions when he saw Louis Colle enjoying himself in a very beautiful garden with other happy youths. He describes himself as being in a kind of distraction and says that the vision lasted but a moment.

Although Louis appeared to Don Bosco many times, he did not appear to his grieving parents who had greatly benefited Don Bosco's work. Finally, Don Bosco asked him why he did not let his parents, who loved him so much, see him. Louis replied that he knew they loved him, but he did not have God's permission to let them see him. Besides, if he spoke directly to them, his words would not be as effective as when they were relayed through Don Bosco.

Don Bosco said of these visions that Louis's face had the same features as when he was alive, except that he looked healthier and happier and he glowed. His clothes sparkled with gold and were the color of lilies and roses. He was dressed differently in the various visions. When Don Bosco asked him for an explanation, Louis said it was simply for the delight of Don Bosco's eyes.

Don Bosco said he had studied about these experiences and felt they were not tricks of the imagination, but real. From what he could see in them, the dreams clearly conformed with the Spirit of God. He said he did not know what God had in mind.

Louis Colle continued to appear to Don Bosco in visions and dreams at least through 1884. He taught him things he did not know about theology and science and God's greatness, and he encouraged him in the work of missions.

Don Bosco's dreams illustrate that dreams of deceased loved ones have many meanings that are unrelated to grief. This does not mean they should be any less valued. They inspire, instruct, warn, reveal just as other dreams. They are also comforting, I think, because the deceased provide this inspiration, instruction, and warning to help the dreamer to get on with his life (vol. 15, 57-70).

PART 3

Other Aspects
of Dreams and Mourning

There does exist a small number of people who obtain knowledge
existing in other people's minds or in the outer world by means as yet
unknown to science. — Gayle Delaney, *Living Your Dreams*

To begin using dreams and dreamwork as a kind of fortune-telling
tool for the benefit of oneself or others is to begin misusing the gift of
dreaming. — Louis Savary, *Dreams and Spiritual Growth: A Christian
Approach to Dreamwork*

This part of the book is an effort to answer questions that often arise in any discussion of dreams: psychical characteristics, non-Western cultural practices, pet appearances, and losses other than by death.

The dreams, explanations, and observations provided here may not answer such questions to your satisfaction, but I hope that discussing them will add to your appreciation of the mysterious nature of dreaming.

10. Dreams in Which Someone Dies

Some dreams have clairvoyant and telepathic qualities and some contain premonitions, but most researchers conclude that the usual purpose of our dreams is give insights into everyday living. We must be careful about taking our dreams too literally. Often when a dreamer dreams about the death of a loved one, the image is actually a metaphor for another life event, not necessarily a death. Dreaming of a parent's death, for example, may in fact be a separation dream that occurs when a young adult makes the transition into an independent life outside the family home. Even when the dream is thought to be precognitive, it can only be verified after the fact.

The Precognitive Dream

Do dreams predict death? These dreams are about something other than bereavement; but since they frequently come up in connection with dreams about deceased persons, I will include them here. When a dream is about a living friend or relative being killed or dying, the dreamer fears that the dream is saying that this is actually going to happen. I had one such dream eight years ago: "I'm doing floor exercises on a wooden platform or deck outside by the lake. Mama is there. To my astonishment she collapses and dies right before my eyes."

If I had not had the experience of working with dreams, I might have been alarmed, thinking this dream predicted her death. I felt surprise more than any other emotion. What was happening was this: I was gaining too much weight, and I needed to lower my cholesterol and triglycerides. I had just completed five days at a rugged, non-pampering fitness spa where I had lost four and one-half pounds by walking, other exercise, and a high fiber, high complex carbohydrate, lowfat diet. I was pleased with the outcome of my visit to the spa. This was the night before Mother's Day, which may have contributed to the mother image. However, my mother is heavy, and I think my losing weight was symbolized in my dream as losing the heavy-Mama part of myself. My dream was saying, "You've done a good job."

A woman in a gathering where I was discussing dreams told me that just the night before, she had dreamed that her husband died. Although she tried to pass it off as just a dream, it bothered her somewhat. She confessed she had become angry with her husband the previous evening. We talked a little about what her life would be like if her husband were to die, and what she would want to do to prepare for such a happening. Maybe the dream was reminding her what life would be like without him, or what she should do in the event of his death. This was not a predictive dream; it was not even a wish-fulfillment dream.

Dr. Bernard S. Siegel, a surgeon at Yale-New Haven Hospital, who uses patients' dreams in the healing process, says the following:

> Don't be too quick to leap to a dire conclusion about the meaning of such dreams (dreams of death or uncontrollable threats to your life). Although I believe that some people do have precognitions of death in their dreams, and I have even delayed surgery in response to a dream of impending death, I think that often we interpret dreams in which death appears too literally. Death can stand for many things besides our own (or our loved ones') actual death (70).

Three writers—Ann Faraday, Phoebe McDonald, and Gayle Delaney—give the following explanations for dreams in which someone dies. Faraday, a pioneer in contemporary dream research, offers this explanation.

> Normally the dreaming mind uses death as a metaphor to express the fact that our feeling for someone, or someone's feeling for us, is dead, or that we have allowed something in our inner life to die....The most interesting dream death is our own, for this indicates the death of some obsolete self-image, from which comes rebirth into a higher state of consciousness and authentic self-being (267).

Phoebe McDonald, a psychoanalytic personal counselor for thirty-some years, says that "while it cannot be denied that certain people have had at times prophetic dreams...it will often be found that the message is entirely different from what it first appeared to be" (11). A few of her examples follow:

- A parent's death may symbolize being freed from over-attachment.

- A wish for a person's death in a dream is really a wish to be rid of problems the person poses.

- Death can symbolize the termination of a relationship or a stage of life (11).

Other dream specialists, such as Gayle Delaney, caution us about taking such dreams literally. She says that death in a dream rarely signifies a warning of a real death. Instead, "death may mean a part of the dreamer represented by the dying person is losing influence in the dreamer's life. This may or may not be desirable, according to the context of the dream" (61). Gayle tells this dream, which reflects the dreamer's letting the creative Barbra Streisand part of herself die:

> I am outdoors, and the world looks green and beautiful. Amid trees and plants, I see Barbra Streisand, lying dead in an open coffin. I feel very sad that she has died. Then

> I wonder if she might not be dead, but in a very deep
> sleep (59).

Prophetic dreams, called *precognitive* dreams in most books about dreams, can only be known after the fact, but there is recognition of them in connection with death.

This dream has a precognitive quality. Ben and his wife began early in their marriage to use their dreams to help them become resources to each other. During the first five years of their marriage, Ben's father had a series of ten or so heart attacks and two cardiac arrests. A year before his father's death, Ben made the following statement:

> I dreamed his death, seeing myself with him, our saying
> goodbye. I then dreamed that I had been unable to
> attend his funeral or to return to my work, because of my
> crying and intense sadness. I told [my wife] that I had
> been unable to attend the funeral as I could not control
> my crying. Then she asked if I had received a call and I
> said no. She then knew that I had been dreaming, only
> she continued to hold me until my sadness passed and
> then she was able to tell me I had been dreaming.
>
> I became aware of my resentment when my
> grandparents died and my parents did not tell me how
> depressed they were, the pain of their loss. I was in pain
> myself, yet they protected me in not sharing their
> sadness. The dream enabled me to talk to each of them
> of their parents' deaths and to learn more details of their
> grief.

Dreams allow us to express sadness by weeping. That the sadness and crying take place before the event of death is unique. However, this happens in waking life when a diagnosis of a terminal illness is made, so why not in dreams?

Here Ben appears to be rehearsing for the end of the unfolding drama of his father's life. The sadness is made more intense perhaps by not having finished mourning for his grandparents when he was young. The dream also helped Ben and his parents share their sadness for their parents—his grandparents.

Predictive dreams seldom speak directly of a particular person's death or of death at all. In the following dream the death of the dreamer is not mentioned directly, but, since it is the last dream of a dying man, it is understood to be about death. The dream provides certainty of resurrection in the image of black birds changing to white when they die.

> At the base of a high rocky wall a huge fire of wood was burning. The flames rose high up into the air and there was much smoke. The place was lonely and romantic. High in the air a number of big black birds dove deliberately into the fire and as each died its color was changed into white (Mahoney 221, 225).

Sometimes approaching death is symbolized by beauty in a dream. The following dream is of this nature:

> I was walking through a beautiful landscape and recognized it as reminiscent of the grounds of the cemetery where my friend had been buried. There came a tall man dressed in a dark black suit who joined me silently. We admired the blue sky, the green grass and the flower beds. We came to a blooming bush which I now recognized as Mountain Lilac. I held my arm underneath it and tapped one branch so that blue blossoms rained on my arm. This was supposed to show my friend (who had died two months previously) that I will join him soon—we all will at the end (Grotjahn 433).

The background of this dream helped the dreamer understand it. On the morning of his death, the dying friend had told him about dreaming of a blue wheelchair. Somehow this dream had helped him reach peace with himself and the world and be able to accept his own death.

Meinrad Craighead's dream is one of such extraordinary beauty that I can scarcely imagine it (61). This incredible dream came to her just a few nights before her mother's sudden death. The dream does not speak of death, and her mother's death was not expected. There is a journey involved. Perhaps she thought of it as representing her own life's journey at the time and did not relate it to her mother's death until afterward. She does not say.

The journey motif came from her childhood. Her grandfather drove a Rock Island train from Little Rock, Arkansas, to Memphis, Tennessee. When she visited her grandparents, he would tell her stories of what he had seen from the engine windows.

In her dream, Meinrad is traveling by train. Her grandfather is in the locomotive driving the train. Memaw, her grandmother, sits alone in the coach behind the engine. The coaches between are empty. They are traveling slowly on a hilly, egg-shaped planet hanging in space. This planet has a rocky landscape pitted with caverns and looks like a solidified sponge. Although Meinrad is on the planet, she can also see it from a distance in space. It looks like an island in a transparent sea of stars. (The way her dream picks up *rocky* and *island* from the name *Rock Island* is fascinating and therefore deals with life's journey.) The train moves on tracks that turn inward, taking them deeper into the caverns that tunnel the planet. From the coach window she sees caves brilliantly illuminated with shining jewels. She tastes something sweet. The sweetness grows. She is tasting the colors of the jewels. She hears the voices of many people chanting:

> The walls are ornate with precious stones of every sort:
> the first is dark green jasper, the second blue sapphire,
> the third grey chalcedony, the fourth green emerald, the
> fifth red sardonyx, the sixth red ruby, the seventh olive
> chrysolite, the eighth blue-green beryl, the ninth yellow
> topaz, the tenth green chrysoprase, the eleventh orange
> jacinth and the twelfth violet amethyst. There are twelve
> gates, each made of a single pearl and paths are of pure
> gold, transparent as glass (61).

Then she realizes she is being carried through the maze of her mother's body. The train slows to a halt, and she is suddenly released out into space among the stars. Now she can see the rocky little planet she has been traveling on and through. It has been transformed into a shining lodestar—a star used to steer by, such as the North Star. She is led by the shining lodestar, which is her mother's shining body, out in the heaven's starry maze.

Taste sensation in dreams is rare and makes the dream special in itself. Another unusual feature is the chant. It is from the book of Revelation in the Bible and part of the description of the Holy City known as the New Jerusalem. A dying person becoming a newborn star is a beautiful image, too.

This dream must have been very comforting to Meinrad after her mother's death. Although it may seem precognitive looking back on it, I wonder if it may not have been a comforting dream given ahead of time. Why not? Dream content does not follow our time frame sequence. Why should the timing of the dream be bound by our timing?

Ugliness, too, can symbolize death. Here is such a dream by a man in a group of terminally ill people:

> I found myself in an office where I had started my career fifty years before. I had been gone for a long time and had not done my duty during this time. Of this I was painfully aware. My former colleagues were very old, sitting silently everywhere, and signing forms. There was dirt and disorder all around. On the papers were standing dirty trays, coffee cups and spoons, and it was disgusting. I discovered that I was barefoot, and I was fearing that I was stepping into filth (Grotjahn 433).

Again, let me caution you about automatically interpreting all dreams of beauty or ugliness as symbolizing death. The things happening in our life at the time of the dream provide the understanding. The dream in which the blue blossoms rained on the dreamer's arm was in the context of a friend's death and his dream before dying. The second dream is in the context of dying people. Whether the dreamer goes to church, is religious, or has no special expectations of the hereafter does not make a difference in whether the dream is symbolized by peace and beauty or ugliness.

Natural catastrophic occurrences often seem to appear in dreams that predict death, but we should not assume that such dreams are always connected with an approaching death. Because it is difficult to determine the precognitive nature of these dreams, we can only be aware that it is a possibility.

A young Swiss woman dreamed of a natural catastrophe the night before her boyfriend had a heart attack. He died three weeks later. Her dream was of an avalanche in the snowcapped Alps. However, her boyfriend had a dream before his death that made no mention of death. He dreamed about a storm that caused pine trees to fall—again, a natural force. One element of the dream did cause him to wonder whether it could be about approaching death. He felt sadness watching lumberjacks carry away the strong trees. Still he considered that it could mean that the effects of his illness must be cleared away, so he could begin life anew. Here are the two dreams:

> *Hers.* An alpine landscape. I am supposed to go to a
> specific place. A shy girl about 16 years old is
> accompanying me. We are following a chain of high
> snowcapped mountains but are ourselves in a green
> meadow. The sun is warm. Suddenly, there is a great
> rumble, an avalanche sweeps rocks and a few trees
> down with it, then hits some farmers' huts below. We are
> a few meters away from the edge of the avalanche. There
> is no danger, but I feel paralyzed. The sun is gone.
> Suddenly the meadow is strangely gray. We go into one
> of the huts which remains standing and still seems to be
> occupied. We must notify the mountain rescue team.
>
> *His.* I see a forest over which a storm must have broken.
> The pines are lying this way and that. Lumberjacks are
> there. They are there. They are loading the trees and
> carrying them away. I wonder why the forest, which
> seems so strong, could not withstand the storm. I watch
> sadly (Kast 21-22, 27).

A Canadian author-farmer writes of finding natural cata-strophic occurrences twenty-one times in his dreams over a thirteen-year period before his father's death. These disasters included a mountain crumbling into an avalanche of stones, floods, earthquakes, and tidal waves. His dream, which follows, was entered in his journal about four years before his father was killed in a farm tractor accident. I would not have expected a precognitive dream so far in advance. Nevertheless, the similarity between the dream event and the actual event is striking.

The dream. I'm standing on the veranda of a house on a snowy morning, overlooking a road that ends as a turnaround place next to a big bank. As I watch in amazement, a white Volkswagen van comes backing down a road to my left which joins onto the turnaround place, fails to stop, and goes hurtling in reverse over the back. Following that, another small truck, a light green Datsun pickup, does the same thing. Thinking that the first one must have Dad in it, I go racing down the hill and find a big pair of rubber boots which I pull on. As I'm doing so, Dad comes struggling up the hill obviously in bad shape. I asked (how) it happened and he mentions about some mechanical problem and says he wants to sit down.

Actual event. My father was thrown off a tractor that rolled backwards over a bank. This happened while he and a neighbor, a younger farmer, were loading gravel onto a truck with the front and bucket of our tractor. Somehow the tractor's brakes failed and the accident followed. After trying desperately to pull the tractor off my father with the truck, the neighbor raced home to get his own bigger tractor, honking his horn and shouting all the way. At our house he slowed down and hollered for my mother to call the ambulance. On his way back down to the accident scene he was followed by another neighbor in a green pickup. A little while later the white ambulance van arrived and swiftly proceeded across the fields toward the accident scene. When they got there, the ambulance attendants saw that my father was dead. Since his death, over four years ago, my wife and I have moved back to the farm. It could be said, at least in part, that as far as running the farm is concerned, I have chosen to fill my father's shoes (R. P. Brown 12).

Dreaming of taking a long journey with an unknown destination and needing no personal property can be a symbol for the journey into death, especially when death is imminent.

The young Swiss man mentioned earlier had this dream before his heart attack.

> The Swiss Army. I am supposed to turn in all my equipment because I am about to undertake a long journey abroad. But I must also hand over my cigarettes, a lighter and a manuscript which I have just begun. I argue that these are my personal property. The officer to whom I must give these things shrugs his shoulders and says, "That's the way it is here: orders are orders." I am looking forward to the journey. At last something unpredictable is happening again (Kast 24).

To turn in military equipment when you take up residence in another country is not unusual. What is unusual is that the dreamer must turn in all his personal things, too. Despite having to leave everything behind, he is looking forward to the journey and experiencing something different. To speak of something new or something longed for even when there is also a feeling of anxiety is typical of such dreams. Be cautious about automatically taking all journey dreams to mean death: The "something new" or different being anticipated may signify something new in this world. Remain open to all possible interpretations. Even then you will not always know, but the context of life when the dream occurs will help with understanding.

Separation Dreams

My niece, Leanne, dreamed that she shot both her parents. Her father was already dead. She did not own a gun nor did she think of using one in her waking life, and she was not on a crusade to assert her independence. However, with her two young children and her husband, Leanne had recently moved from the city where she had grown up. This dream was saying how it felt to her to put considerable distance between herself and her parents' home. It was as if she were killing the parental influence in her life.

What she had was a separation dream. As we establish our own lives and become independent of our parents, we sometimes have such dreams. Sometimes the concern is not just physical distance. The breaking of emotional ties, too, can bring the feeling of separation.

To move away from what has been familiar is scary and sad even when there is the quality of adventure. Our dreams reflect this, and in a way they are like grief dreams.

When a mother or father loses control in our lives or when there is a transition from the role of son or daughter to that of spouse and then parent, we may have a dream in which one or both parents die. In her book *A Time to Mourn,* Verena Kast uses this fseparation dream as an example (139): The dreamer is a thirty-five-year-old man who had married a woman who was not to his mother's liking. He had three children. In the dream he is going to a funeral service in the church. Mourners are there. His wife and three children are with him. His brothers are there with their wives, and he thinks of his father as being there somewhere. He looks for his mother. He is told she has died of a heart attack, and the funeral is being held for her. He is sad but thinks this is not a bad way to die.

The wife and children appearing with the dreamer are depicting a transition from son to husband and parent. The mother was an overly controlling parent. Her death in the dream refers to his realization that the time had come for him to resist this domination and assume his adult roles. Judith Viorst discusses in *Necessary Losses* this natural process of becoming an individual separate from parents and how it can unconsciously feel as if we are killing our parents. She quotes Hans Loewald (160):

> By establishing inner restraints (instead of needing our parents to serve as our external conscience), by cutting emotional ties (instead of seeking our gratifications within the family), by taking care of our needs (instead of surrendering that care to our mother and father), we annihilate our parents' roles and take them onto ourself.

And, in that sense, we are guilty of killing our parents (Loewald 757).

My niece's dream was not predicting aggressive action against her parents. It was simply depicting the change taking place in her life and how it made her feel, on a subconscious level, as if she had actually killed her parents.

Clairvoyant and Telepathic Dreams

Many people have shared their dreams of someone's death that include clairvoyant and telepathic qualities, and I have also read similar accounts of such dreams. For this reason I think they must be rather common. The dream experience occurs at the time of death and not before, so the dream cannot be predictive. Mavis, a missionary friend, once had such an experience when her brother died. She was on another continent.

Sometimes the dreams do not even indicate whose death is being considered. In Mobile, Alabama, on March 21, 1981, Beulah Mae Donald woke from a dream at 2:00 A.M.. She had dreamed there was a steel gray casket in her living room, but she could not tell who the dead man laid out in a gray suit was. She discovered that her nineteen-year-old son, Michael, was not in his bedroom. He had gone to his cousin's. So she called his house and learned that Michael had left for home before midnight. At 7:00 A.M. Mrs. Donald's telephone rang, and she received the message that her son's body had been found dangling from a rope in a tree. The FBI investigation revealed that this brutal murder by members of the Ku Klux Klan took place around the time of Mrs. Donald's dream (Kornbluth).

A mother's telepathic-like dream of her baby and her own mother prepared her for her mother's death.

> This dream occurred on December 9, 1944. Our baby had died suddenly on November 29, 1942, at the age of four months. In my dream (I was asleep) I saw a young woman of about thirty grasping the hand of a small boy just learning to walk. I knew instantly that the boy was ours although both figures faced away from me. I noticed

his sturdy legs particularly. They were running freely and happily up a gentle green slope dotted with flowers—the color of the latter are indescribable—they were not of this world.

The young woman wore a loose dress of indeterminate color, with a girdle at the waist. I felt very close to her. I thought that she was someone very near to me.

I awakened my husband to tell him of my dream because it was so vivid, and I got such great comfort from it. I said, "I believe that was my grandmother with our baby, because she is taking care of him." I felt very happy. My husband noted the time—one-thirty A.M.

The next morning I received a telegram that my mother had died at 1:30 A.M. Having had that dream, I went through the funeral with never a thought of grief—I have never grieved for my mother or baby since (Sanford 63-64).

A rector of an Episcopal church reports the above dream in his writing. He says of it:

We do not know how to interpret the symbols of the hill, the flowers and the age of the little boy in the dream. They point to the continuance of life in another reality…. We can point to two indisputable facts: first, that the dream occurred at the same time as the death of the dreamer's mother; second, that it brought an irrational but profound reassurance. [This dream] "…demonstrates that the unconscious source of our dreams is not necessarily limited by space and time as is our conscious mind…." (Sanford 64).

At first reading this seemed like a clairvoyant or telepathic dream. A *clairvoyant* dream presents the dreamer with information that he or she did not know. In a *telepathic* dream actual events take place at the moment of dreaming about them. This dream does not fall into either category. The time of this comforting and beautiful dream about dear ones who had previously died and the time of her mother's death do come together. This special set of circumstances gives the dream a quality of *synchronicity,* which happens when seemingly random events come together in a meaningful way. Such dreams are called *psychic*; they seem even more mysterious than our regular dreams, which usually convey a sense of mystery as do some waking experiences.

Bernard Siegel tells this mystical story:

> ...the girl's mother was driving down the road when a seagull swooped down and sat in front of her car, causing her to slam on the brakes and wait what seemed like an eternity while the bird took its time sauntering across the road. Her dead daughter's favorite bird was a seagull and somehow she felt that it was Patty come to visit her. Her feeling that there had been some kind of divine intervention with that seagull was soon to be confirmed. When she proceeded down the road once the bird had crossed, she found a horrible car accident at the next corner that she would certainly have been involved in had it not been for the dawdling seagull (225).

This story is not a dream experience, but it is mysterious in the way dreams are. Sometimes we are reluctant to share such dreams and experiences, because we think we will be thought strange and because others may feel uncomfortable hearing them. We need not be so reluctant. These experiences are more common than most people know. Sharing them frees others to share such moments and dreams. This is healing to both the storyteller and the listener.

Premonitory Dreams

Premonition (forewarning) is a puzzling element in many dreams. Most researchers have concluded that the usual purpose of our dreams is to give insights into daily living, and they should be considered first from that viewpoint. Once that is done, the dreamer may discover that the dreams are the result of impressions and information gathered during the day while he or she was too preoccupied with other things to give them attention.

Then there are dreams that appear to convey warnings of a serious, catastrophic nature. The only way we can really know whether a dream is using the image as a metaphor to deal with an everyday matter or is predicting the future is after the warning has come to pass.

As I write this, a premonitory dream has been reported in the newspaper. Jennifer Weston, a college student from Indiana who had gone with her cousin to Texas for the summer, was found stabbed to death along with her cousin. Just the week before, a long-time friend had this frightening dream about Jennifer.

> She came to me and she said she was getting ready to leave and I wouldn't see her again. I kept hugging her and hugging her and crying. I kept crying, "Don't leave me. Don't leave me. You can't do this."
>
> I was so upset I woke up and I was crying....I had this horrible feeling (Hall H1).

Sometimes the dead appear to warn of danger. Mrs. Aniela Jaffe, secretary to Carl Jung and executive secretary of the Jung Institute in Zurich, tells of this story: Her son's life was saved because of his dreams of his dead father for two successive nights in which he was warned, "You may not go over the bridge." The son was in recruit school. He was scheduled to go on maneuvers with his comrades the day after the second dream. That morning he woke up with a fever and could not go. The same day a bridge collapsed resulting in several deaths and injuries of his comrades (Jaffe 34, 36).

Sometimes these warnings are about behavior that may result in serious consequences if it is not changed. However, the warnings appear to point to the inevitable and could also be called prophetic.

Premonitions are not limited to dreams. Often they come during waking time in the form of inexplicable, uneasy feelings that cannot be shaken.

Lydia, a young woman I knew, had what I call a precognitive warning in the form of a vision. She described this experience as a feeling of being surrounded by darkness and seeing moving pictures. She saw everybody and everything she loved taken from her one at a time by death. To her this was depicting her own holocaust. This dream occurred soon after she was married.

Four years later her holocaust began. When her first child was born, Lydia was given a blood transfusion because of complications with her labor and the possibility that a cesarean section might be needed. As it turned out, the delivery was normal and the transfusion had not been needed after all. After three years of unexplainable and unusual illnesses that she, her first child, and by then her second child had suffered constantly, she received a phone call. She was told she had been given blood contaminated with the AIDS virus.

Living in a fearful, unsympathetic society while dying was a terrible and lonely ordeal, although there were individuals who were sympathetic and compassionate. The baby was the first to die, and even the funeral director could not bring himself to touch the body. After that, her father, with whom she had been very close, died of a heart attack.

The daily drudgery of painful treatments for an illness with no possible cure was very draining both physically and psychologically. Yet, before she died, Lydia managed to form a support group of HIV women, take in children whose HIV mothers were too sick to care for them, open a day care facility for children with HIV parents, and nurse (she had been a psychiatric nurse) mothers and children with AIDS. Lydia transcended the inevitable with courage and lived out her destiny with dignity.

Some explain the coming to pass of prophetic and premonitory dreams and experiences as self-fulfilling, but that does not seem so in Lydia's case. It is difficult to understand the value of a warning when nothing can be done to change the outcome. Perhaps it served some purpose that she, or at least we, are not able to identify.

Jung called some dreams *prospective* as opposed to prophetic. Prospective dream content may coincide with actual happenings but does not agree in detail as prophetic dreams do. Louis Savary and his colleagues suggest that "the dream is probably given to us as an informative gift to help prepare us for an event" (215). Neither of these ideas explain Lydia's premonitory vision to my satisfaction.

11. Mourning Dreams in Non-Western Cultures

In some countries and cultures people do not seem to connect the dreams of deceased family members with mourning. At least they do not report dreams that comfort them and help them accept their loss. This may be due to the differences between a Western and a non-Western world view. In many places a dream is taken seriously, depending on who appears in it and what themes predominate. Three types of people appear in dreams—the living, ancestors, and the deceased. Divinities may also appear. However, ancestors and the deceased are dreamed of most often. Other themes can combine with the appearances of the dead, such as human needs, special callings, the naming of a baby, and warnings (Hayashida, "Significance of Dreams," 286).

By emphasizing what can be experienced through the senses or measured by instruments, Western technology and Christian teachings have affected how seriously many people consider dreams. When people from another country or culture accept the Christian tradition, they often feel that they must renounce their former belief systems and traditions. Dreams are often one of the elements they give up. They may feel that dreams are not valued in Christianity, because many Christians give so little significance to them.

A Zambian once complained, "When I asked about the dreams in the Bible, they [missionaries] could not give me the answers. I was very much puzzled....But they said, 'These are only dreams'" (Hayashida, "Significance of Dreams," 287). This is unfortunate because dreams and visions were highly valued in Biblical times. Precautions were taken to use dreams and visions correctly to the glory of God (Deut 13:1-5, 18:9-22; Mic 3:5-7). Consequently, I think missionaries who respond in this way are missing an opportunity to use existing culture to enhance understanding of the Bible. To consider dreams in the Bible as only ancient religious experiences is to refuse to accept part of the Bible as the inspired word of God that has been given for all time. To say that God is not in our sleeping experiences, as well as in our waking ones, is to belittle our dreams and to limit God.

Dreams have been shared freely with me in several places where I've traveled and lived for brief periods. At the time I was not thinking of writing this book and did not document them. My memory does not do them justice, so I will not try to repeat them here. There is, however, one I recall. Actually I recall only the action taken as a result of the dream.

A young Chinese couple from Taiwan shared the husband's dream about his deceased father soon after his death. The content of the dream was interpreted as encouragement to the Christian ministry. When they told me about the dream, they were studying in a seminary in the United States. I had lived a short time in Taiwan and knew that dreams of a deceased parent or ancestor were very important until conversion to Christianity, at which time the new converts usually forsook their dreams. Despite the confusion about dreams in the Christian faith, many do pay attention to them.

Nelson Hayashida has studied the significance of dreams in Zambia and confirms the importance given to dreams involving ancestors in the African culture. Usually when a deceased loved one appears in a dream, it is to give instruction, explanation, or information on matters of importance to the family. Hayashida does not discuss mourning dreams as such, but I have found that the dreamer appears to be comforted by some of the dreams. I give a few of the dreams from his study here.

William Lungu's deceased brother appeared in a dream giving words of comfort and encouragement. According to Hayashida, William, age forty-five, had followed Western religious tradition for thirty-two years at the time of this dream. He had been a deacon and a treasurer of his church for fifteen years and worked as head messenger at Barclays Bank. He was married with eight children. This background information illustrates that despite following a more Western tradition, he still considered dreams important and helpful in matters relating to his family. This is his dream and part of the interview that followed:

> My second-born brother whom I was staying with in Matero passed away in 1962. Some three or four times I dreamed that he was coming to me, talking to me, telling me that he accepted my Lord. He said, "I don't see why you should bear this problem alone." I shared with my wife and my friends. Some say, "He wants you to go where he is." I said, "No, it is not true. That man he has great love. Maybe he comes because I think about him. But I don't think he wants to take me." I had many problems, looking after the children, looking after my mother. I think he feels guilty he has left me all alone with these family problems.
>
> I: So he comes from time to time to give you comfort?
> L: Yes.
> I: Have you found other dead ancestors coming back to give you good advice?
> L: Not really. Only this one brother (288-89).

When he was twenty-one years old, Hamilton Nkoma told this dream to Hayashida. Hamilton had been a Christian for five years and was active in his church as the director of the Sunday school, the treasurer, and a member of the choir. When Hamilton was twelve, his father died. His mother awakened him in the middle of the night when she found his father outside unconscious. He said, "Later I had a dream. I saw my father coming to me. He said, 'Hamilton, you are grown up. Look after your brothers and sisters'" (288-89).

He did not understand what his father meant, so he kept it to himself. As time went by he began to understand that by "being the second born in the family, my father was showing me the risk I had ahead of me" (288-89). The firstborn was a boy and should have been the responsible son in his culture, but he was not present at the time his father died. The words in the dream did not need interpretation. But since the directions were different from the practice in his culture, it took some time for Hamilton to fully comprehend the dream and take it into his life. Would it not comfort a young son to receive guidance and support from his dead father?

Naming a new baby for a dead ancestor who appears in a dream is a common practice in Africa. This tradition makes the child more fully a member of society and connected with the community of the past. Although this practice does not deal with bereavement, I include it because it is a use of dreams about the deceased. I think this may be comforting to the child as well as the parents.

Paul Bwembya Mushindo, a Zambian evangelist now deceased, told this story about his naming: When his birth was near, the king, Citimokula Bwembya, appeared to Kapalyo (his mother) in a dream and said, "I am King Citimokula Bwembya. I have come to stay with you, my daughter" (Mushindo 4-5). When the baby was born, he was named Bwembya.

12. Dreams of
Bereaved Pet Owners

Entire books are being published on the subject of pet loss. One such book, *Pet Loss* by Herbert Nieburg and Arlene Fisher, reminds us that "grief is not a feeling that is reserved for loss of friends or relatives. Grief is a normal reaction whenever we undergo an important loss of any kind....Grief specialists observe that people often respond to human loss and pet loss in similar ways....Crying and feeling lonely or depressed are natural ways of responding to the death of a cat or dog that has shared one's daily life" (2, 9-10).

According to Jamie Quakenbush and Denise Graveline, authors of *When Your Pet Dies*, "professionals have been able to observe firsthand the depth and range of pet owners' grief and mourning and know that it is comparable to the process following human death" (19). Quakenbush and Graveline are with the Veterinary Hospital of the University of Pennsylvania. Some of the suggestions in their book for adjusting to the loss of a pet may help you understand dreams you may have about your deceased pet.[1]

---

1 Paraphrases and quotations from pages 19-59; my emphasis in italics.

- *What to do when others do not understand your grief for a pet.* A complicating factor is that "it's still not acceptable to be upset by an animal's death, so you face not only private sorrow but public bereavement made difficult by other's attitudes. Some will be sympathetic and others won't. *You can ask them to respect your sorrow or you might just avoid them for a while.*" To grieve alone for a time before you share your feelings may be helpful.

- *How to accommodate to life without your pet.* "You've lost a lifestyle as well as a friend," so, "*plan to gradually alter your routine.*" You may have walked your dog every day rain or shine or you may have been greeted by your cat when you returned home from work. You can still walk, maybe with a friend or listen to music to keep down the loneliness at first. You can let something else demand your attention when you first come home—such as watering your houseplants.

- *Helping your pet to die.* You have had to aid in your pet's death "when your caring acts can no longer keep him [or her] alive" or from pain in the last days. *Take comfort from these words: "You're able only to do everything you can—and no more."*

- *What to do with the sadness you keep experiencing.* "Whenever you lose something that plays a central role in your life—whether it's a spouse, a friend, a job, a livelihood, a skill, or your pet" you may feel bad and unable to take pleasure in what you do. This is normal. *Let sadness run its course.*

- *Figure out what kind of companion your pet was.* "As you recall all the moments you shared, you'll understand your reaction to his [or her] death and discover the true worth of his [or her] contribution to your life." Finding and acknowledging clues to your pet's significant role in your life can help you

understand yourself better, as well as help you
adjust to life without your pet.

Besides pleasure, what else did your pet provide?
Protection? Cats, as well as dogs, can alert us when
something they are not used to is going on. My cat
can sense someone coming down the street before
I'm aware of it. My dog becomes alarmed when
more containers of trash than usual are put out to
be picked up. Acceptance? Pets don't argue with
you. They pay attention to your slightest glances,
to your affectionate hugs._They can't interrupt,
contradict or betray." Reliability? A pet is a constant
factor in a rapidly changing life. A pet's constant
presence may come very close to being as
reassuring as companionship with a human friend.
The pet's always being there may even help you
feel better able to handle disappointments and
difficult transitions. Inviting you to play their
favorite game and spurring you on when life does
not seem meaningful may have helped you, the
owner, feel wanted.

I am pleased that books on grieving, such as *Grieving* by
Therese Rando and *Dreams That Can Change Your Life* by Alan
Siegel, are beginning to discuss the human-pet bond and the
grief involved.

Rando recognizes grief for a deceased pet as a situation that
is not socially acknowledged. This is an area where there needs
to be better understanding of the importance of grieving. Siegel
writes, "The death of a cherished pet can be profoundly upsetting
and may trigger a grieving process that closely resembles the
grief we might feel for a close friend or relative" (257).

Bereavement dreams can occur with grieving, whether it is a
beloved person or a beloved animal that dies. However, bereaved pet owners do not tend to share their dreams. I suspect
they dream of their beloved animal companions; but they do
not feel safe in sharing these dreams any more than they would
share their pain for any loss that is not socially recognized. I have

included three dreams from my reading, two of my own and one of my husband's. I think they illustrate how dreams of bereaved pet owners are very much like those of people who grieve for dead loved ones.

Pet Deaths Help Dreamers Grieve Other Losses

When Barbara had the following dream, she was on a wilderness backpacking trip. Barbara was camping near a mountain in California called Pico Blanco, which is considered a sacred site by the Ohlone Indians. According to legend, the tribe began on this mountain with a mythical coyote after surviving a great flood. This legend partially explains the dream's use of the image of the coyote, but Barbara's exploration of it gives a more personal meaning.

> There is a wild dog nearby, maybe a wolf or coyote. I lie
> still because I'm not sure if it will attack me. Somehow I
> fall back to sleep and wake up (still in the dream) and
> when I awaken the dog is lying asleep on my chest
> (A. Siegel 258).

As Barbara told her dream to the group she was with, she began to associate it not only with the coyote legend, but with her dog, Emily, as well. Emily, a mixed breed who looked a little like a coyote, had recently died. But since it is not socially acceptable to be upset by an animal's death, Barbara had not said anything about her grief. My experience is that a person who expresses sadness at the loss of a pet is considered "silly" or "weak" or lacking a sense of perspective.

The strangeness of the wild coyote sleeping peacefully on Barbara's chest could be a metaphor for the heaviness of the sadness (heavy-heartedness) she felt for her own dead pet. The loneliness of not having someone with whom to share her sadness added weight to her grief. However, Barbara found herself feeling the pain of another loss as she further explored the loss of her nurturing relationship with her dog. She was letting go of the hope of ever having a child to nourish, because she was at an age when she would not likely conceive.

So Barbara's dream helped her understand the nurturing nature of her pet-human bond and mourn for her pet. In addition, the dream helped her acknowledge grief for children she would not have and express it with the caring members of the group.

Sylvia's dream of her pet's death helped her mourn her son's death. Experiencing the death of a pet before recovering from a previous loss can aid in mourning that resolves both deaths. Dreams accompany these experiences, too. Here is one such story from my reading.

The dreamer had suffered the loss of a son through suicide. Sammy, the family dog, had died of cancer a year after Sylvia and Bill's son, Paul, took his life in his struggle with depression. Relatives had been so shocked that they avoided discussing the tragedy. Sylvia and one of her daughters decided to travel across the United States to visit relatives. They intended to discuss and grieve the son's death openly.

One night during these visits, Sylvia dreamed of both Sammy and Paul:

> Bill and I were dragging a coffin into our living room. I looked in. There was Sammy. His dog form known to me. I was a bit shocked because I was sure it would be Paul. I ran my eyes over him, the ears, the spots, the flank, the tail, the paws. Dear Sammy. I turned away, and when I looked again, the body was no longer Sammy, but Paul as we found him. It was the whole suicide scene, just exactly as he was lying there, except he was in the coffin _ As before, I ran my eyes over the beloved boy. The body was clothed, and I paused at the hips, wondering if the lipoma from his childhood was still there. I looked for a while at the body as though from a distance of time. And it wasn't nightmare horrible, as at the time of death. When I awoke I immediately knew the meaning of the dream. We have brought the death into the living room. And we can live with it. I awoke satisfied that the dream reflected the truth (Zimmerman 50).

Sylvia's dream used Sammy's death to focus her attention on Paul's death. She needed to look at it from the distance of time after the immediate grief had passed. This was not a distance of avoidance. She had moved on with her life by visiting relatives and helping them accept her horrible loss. Her dream helped her know that this was right for her. It gave her courage to move on with her life. She could even remember the good times of living with her son and growing up with him.

Dream Replaces Unpleasant Memories with Comforting Ones

Mary had the following dream three days after reluctantly having to end her nineteen-year-old cat's suffering. Snowflake was blind, deaf, and weak. Mary carefully wrapped her in a towel and took her to the veterinary hospital. As they entered the hospital, Snowflake had a seizure and bit Mary. This was a terribly upsetting way to end a loving relationship with a pet.

> I was in the hallway of my apartment and there was Snowflake. She looked healthy and was as affectionate as ever.
>
> I thought to myself, "That's great but what happened?" I called the hospital and the vet told me that several of them tried to do something to save her but in the end they gave up and just left the doors open (the implication being that she just got up and walked out).
>
> I felt so good to see her. As soon as I awoke, I realized that what I had done was to replace an ugly image with this comforting one (Ullman and Zimmerman 151).

This dream helped Mary replace the unpleasant memories of her cat's suffering and last moments with positive memories that were more characteristic of her life with Snowflake. Also, her dream reassured her that her cat was free from suffering; it made accepting her loss easier.

Dream Relieves Guilt

When I moved from Texas to California, I had to leave my twelve-year-old German Shepherd, Ralph. He was in good condition for a dog his age, so we could not bring ourselves to end his life; but we also could not keep pets in the apartment in California. I thought we were fortunate when we found a nice home for Ralph, but he did not live long. I felt sad when I learned of his death. He had been faithful and devoted to me, even warning my husband and me when a stranger entered our home. The following dream still makes me smile after sixteen years.

> Ralph comes bounding toward me. He has grown one
> antler and has another coming. The antler looks more
> like what I think a moose antler looks like. I laugh and
> play with him. When I start to feed him, I discover he is
> about out of food. I give him what dry dog food there is
> and tell him I'll go to the store and get him some canned
> food. Then I open a can of apple pie for myself and,
> forgetting what I'm doing, put it in his dish. He's eating it
> before I can do anything about it. I pat him on the neck
> and tell him that I'll get him some apple pie too, if he
> likes it so well.

Antlers and changing food-likes suggest a transformation. Antlers add beauty and majesty to the male moose and deer. To me, the moose is more of a humorous creature, but majestic nevertheless. Until he was grown, Ralph had one ear that flopped over. It always made me laugh, because he looked like a big, floppy-eared bunny. My dream was saying that in death my dog was being transformed into an even more majestic animal, but he still had the endearing quality of a floppy ear in the form of one antler not having grown. His bounding to me was typical of his affectionate nature and his devotion to me, and despite my having to leave him, he held no grudge. The dream helped me think of Ralph with affection instead of only pain. It gave me the pleasure of being with him, even though I knew he was no longer living. The guilt I felt for abandoning him gave way to pleasant memories of his playfulness and loyalty. I still feel warm and smiling inside when I think of him.

A Waking-Up Dream Confirms a Change in Daily Routine

When it became clear that twelve-year-old Nicholas, suffering from arthritis and a congenital hip condition, was in considerable pain and could not be helped to get on his feet or walk, I called his veterinarian. He assured me that nothing more could be done. I called my husband who was out of town, and our son who lived in another city. We all sadly agreed it was not right to let him suffer further.

His veterinarian came to the house as I could not lift such a large dog into the car. It was a beautiful Kentucky autumn day. Yellow leaves gently fell around us on the green grass in the backyard that Nicholas loved so much. That is where we were when his veterinarian arrived. I stroked Nicholas's beautiful black wavy fur, which glistened in the sunlight, and as he was given an injection in his front leg, I told him we were not going to let him hurt any more. In an instant I felt him let go of his pain—and his life. Shock—at realizing that what was alive an instant ago was forever gone from the world" interrupted the sadness of having to make this decision. Charles Dickens's words describe my feelings so accurately: "And can it be that in a world so full and busy, the loss of one weak creature makes a void in my heart, so wide and deep that nothing but the width and depth of vast eternity can fill it up" (242).

Five days later, just before waking up, I dreamed the following:

> Nicholas is at my bedside nosing me to get up. He sits
> back to await my getting up to let him outside. I open my
> eyes expecting to see him and remember immediately
> that he is dead.

This was the way our days began. When he heard the bells from the nearby church and school, Nicholas knew that he could go outside. If I was not already up, he would awaken me. Some material I have read on grief would call this dream a form of denial of the death, but I experienced it as forgetfulness. This habit of many years had caused me to forget momentarily, as I was beginning to awaken, that Nicholas was no longer there to be let out. However, I was surprised at how physically real the feeling of his nose nudging me was. I think it was the expectation of the daily ritual exaggerated by the dream. The contrast of Nicholas's presence in my dream with waking reality helped me get used to his absence. It was as if I had to relive many times his not being there until my daily routine without him could be changed.

Euthanasia Contaminates Scheduled Surgery in Dream

My husband, Bill, had a disturbing dream a month after Nicholas's death and the day before he was to have surgery. Anxiety over the surgery seemed to be more the concern of this dream than grief for Nicholas.

In a previous surgery Bill had overheard his anesthesiologist say, "He's not coming out of it," which he took to mean he wasn't going to live. Because of this experience Bill was apprehensive about using general anesthesia, although he had chosen it instead of local anesthesia. Nevertheless, he thought he would dislike more knowing what was going on during the surgery. Now Bill was having second thoughts. The account of Nicholas's death in my dream experience shows how the veterinarian and anesthesiologist became associated in Bill's dream:

> The anesthesiologist comes. Nicholas is friendly and
> happy to see him and paws at him the way he does
> when he wants attention and wants to be petted. At first I
> see Nicholas with his head blurred, almost as if he didn't
> have a head, and wet like a newborn puppy. Although
> his body didn't show signs of this, I think of him as
> having had his viscera removed because he is an organ
> donor. As Nicholas paws at the anesthesiologist, I see
> only his paw. His paw caused a problem because it gets
> the doctor's paraphernalia dirty. The doctor gives the

> impression of being an orthopedic doctor whom I had
> gone to years ago and is no longer living.

Bill thought of Nicholas as having died in the dream. The blurred head reminds me of how sometimes people cannot see the face of the deceased loved one in either waking conscious memory or in dreams immediately after the death. Bill felt anxious over the upcoming surgery, although "wet like a newborn puppy" suggests a birth and "organ donor" suggests giving health and well being.

There is an association of the anesthesiologist inserting the needle in Bill's wrist with the veterinarian giving Nicholas a lethal injection into his foreleg. What had happened to Nicholas made what the anesthesiologist was preparing to do (give anesthesia for surgery) seem bad or "dirty." But upon reflection, what the doctor would do for Bill was to make him well. Bill's doctor's purpose was different from the veterinarian's. The dead pet/organ donor, the doctor who was no longer living, and the contamination of the surgical equipment made Bill think the dream was warning him that the outcome did not look good.

I understood the dream differently. Our dog had been a source of much pleasure which promoted our well being, especially by keeping us faithful in taking our daily walks. An organ donor contributes life to the recipient. The doctor, who was no longer living, had been a compassionate physician who was concerned for his patients. So it seemed that all the positive elements in the dream indicated only a good outcome.

The surgery went well. The meaning of the dream is still not clear to Bill. I include the dream because it illustrates how dreams of deceased pets may be concerned with other things occurring in the life of the dreamer at the time.

13. Dream Benefits

We have seen that experiencing bereavement dreams can provide a variety of benefits to the dreamer. Dreams can provide comfort and help resolve other issues in life. Dreams can move the dreamer through the grieving process and can help the dreamer deal with losses other than death. Dreams can also alleviate the changes that occur as a result of loss, and they can bring personal issues and special memories to the attention of the dreamer.

Dreams Provide a Resource for Comfort and for Resolution of Other Problems

That some people do not seem to have mourning dreams should not make them feel deprived. Nor should those who experience such dreams feel privileged. People who do not experience mourning dreams may not need them or their needs may be met in another way. We do not know why some people recall dreams and others do not. We do not know why some people dream of their dead loved ones while others, even those who may recall dreams ordinarily, do not. Dreams are mysterious by nature. Actually dreams are a function of our own bodies, and there is much about all of our body functions and processes that remains mysterious. The more we discover about dreams, the more there is still left to learn. Nevertheless, dreams provide a resource for comfort and resolving other problems surrounding a loss. They will benefit the dreamer who gives consideration to them. They are especially helpful when a person gets mired in the grieving process.

Dreams Move the Dreamer through the Grieving Process

Joe recognized through his dreams that he was stuck in the process of grieving for his mother. Twelve years after her death, he was still dreaming about her and waking up in fresh grief all over again. This was followed by feelings of guilt and wanting his mother's forgiveness. One day Joe realized that this pattern of grieving was leading to anger and overwork. It was even affecting the motivation for his ministry as a prison chaplain. That day he took his coffee cup, on which his mother had painted his name, and *disenchanted* it. He made it like any other cup by putting it aside instead of using it as an object to help keep her alive. He even conducted his own personal funeral for her, saying simply, "Rest in peace, Mother."

Joe's waking up in grief after his unpleasant dreams indicate he had not been able to let go of his mother on an emotional level. When he stopped trying to keep her alive, he no longer needed dreams to nudge him to continue his grieving to a resolution.[1]

When grief does not progress, difficulties can occur. Probably most of us have known people who have tried to fill the void of loneliness, meaningless, emptiness, and longing with drugs, alcohol, food, work, sex, or even war and danger. Grief can be avoided for only so long. Finally, it erupts and is expressed in destructive or unhealthy ways. When a grieving person develops self-destructive behavior such as overwork, addiction, or relationship problems, grief is not being worked through and resolved. Joe says that the severe drug and alcohol abuse of

---

1 This dream experience was reported by a chaplain in a state penitentiary who participated in a dream study group I was facilitating.

forty-five percent of the inmates he interviews started with a severe loss through a death or divorce. These people usually had not accepted their loss. His own experience with his mother's death helped him recognize this truth. The person must be allowed to die. "One day—an idea that will horrify you now—this intolerable misfortune will become a blessed memory of a being who will never again leave you" (Proust).

Dreams are a wonderful way to help you store your memories. The first dream my sister recalls came after our Uncle Tommy's death. She was eleven years old when Tommy was killed instantly in a car wreck. She was enough to have remembered what he looked like; yet, she says she has no recollection of him except from this dream and pictures. He appeared so vividly that she even remembers the texture and color of his hair and that his eyes were hazel-green. He was grinning (that's the way we all remember him) and said, "I'm happy now." Her memory of the way he looked fits pictures she saw of him later.

Dreams Help with Losses of All Kinds

Dreams also reflect losses other than the death of a family member, a friend, or a pet. Although these dreams are not the focus of this book, I mention them because they often express the same feelings of sadness and distress rather intensely.

I had a dream recently in which lost objects represented the way I used to be—my youthful self. I am searching for missing baby clothes when I realize that the baby is missing. Then, I dream my memory is gone, and the doctor tells me that nothing can be done. I am really distressed when I wake up. I call this my Lost Youth dream because the part of me who wore youthful clothes is gone. Even the clothes are gone.

This dream pictures what shopping for clothes is like to me sometimes. I see these cute things that young girls wear. Clothes are so much more attractive now than when I was young, but they would not be appropriate for my social occasions or lifestyle. It is sometimes a dilemma to shop for clothes that do not look "oldish" and at the same time do not look too young.

The dream slips in a little humor here as it seems to be saying that my shopping is like looking for baby clothes. Why not honor your age? The lost memory part is more serious. The first part of the dream seems to be saying, "Because you've lost your youth, your memory is a problem, also. Just accept that as you would any other loss, as a part of living." Still, I am not so sure I want to accept my "dream doctor's" advice. I think I will work at finding ways to compensate for the loss and techniques for improving my memory or keeping what I have. Maybe further dreams will shed some light on this subject.

Fifteen years earlier, I had a dream in which I was absolutely prostrate with grief. I was puzzled about the expression of such great grief over a loss that should probably pass as little more than a feeling of disappointment. After all, it was just the loss of a choice—or was it? What is really puzzling is why I had the dream in San Juan where I was working with preschool children for a week. The setting and activities did not show up in the dream as daily residue. So I decided it must be about my mother or the mother part of me, maybe even something of a broader, more all-encompassing nature. Then I noticed the date. I had had the dream on my birthday. I called it Circle of Grief.

> I am watching a beauty contest with others in our living room. Our favorite candidate lost. Suddenly, as though she were dead, everyone falls to the floor. They stretch out completely on the floor with their faces down and their feet and legs straight out behind them with their heads positioned toward the center. They are in great grief with much crying and sobbing. I feel so sad. Yet, it feels I need to help them somehow. Food is brought in. I prepare it for serving, but nobody would come to eat. My mother comes in. She does not seem to know about the result of the contest, or to be grieving. She is pretty, and young, and moving gracefully. She looks as young as when I was a little girl. I ask her if she didn't know what happened. I feel a little stunned that she did not seem sad. She said, "Tell them we are ready to eat, and that we

will eat now." I am confused that they are so grieved and
she has so little concern for their grief.

The children and other workers had celebrated my birthday
with cake and punch. We all had a good time, but something
else must have been going on in my mind. Dreams are usually
about the dreamer. Two features I had been proud of were my
naturally wavy, rich brown hair and pretty ankles. Now my
thinning hair was mostly gray and my ankles hurt as did other
joints. I am not sure why my mother appears pretty and young
as when I was a little girl. Maybe this part pictures the feeling of
wanting to be mothered as if I were that little girl. Being with
young children that week may have been the source of this
image, so there may be a suggestion of current daily life here—a
bit of daily residue. The stern mother of my dream is saying, "Life
must go on."

Grief regarding lost careers or a lost way of life can be dealt
with in dreams. One such dream shared with me illustrates both
of these: Terry had gone into the Marines at the same time as his
cousin. His father and all of his uncles were Marines, and he and
his cousin were following this proud family tradition. When the
time came for Terry to go into combat, his physical showed a
heart condition and he was discharged. He became the first
person in his family to attend college. Nevertheless, he had lost
a way of life, and the new way of life was not yet clear. His health
problem may have been a source of distress, causing him to lose
his good self-image.

In a recurrent dream he saw a book, like a college yearbook,
with his Marine buddies' pictures in it. Each page carried a single,
very small picture with captions like *wounded* and *missing in
action.* His own picture always appeared large and on the last
page with the caption *college student.* This dream, picturing him
as one of the war casualties, gave evidence of his distress and
disturbed him as well. An observing professor, noticing his
anxiety, initiated a conference that resulted in a resolution to the
problem and led Terry into a music career. After that, he had no
more dreams showing him and his Marine friends as casualties.

Dreams Alleviate Changes Experienced As Loss

Vamik D. Valkan, a Cypriot Turk, came to the United States after medical school to take an internship in a Chicago hospital. He is now a psychiatrist and psychoanalyst living in Virginia as an American citizen.

Valkan and a friend undertook the project of writing a psychobiography of Ataturk, the father of modern Turkey. The death of Valkan's own Turkish father in Cyprus, the political unrest that endangered the lives of his family and friends there at the time, and the relinquishment of his Cypriot Turkish culture were lingering issues that had not been completely laid to rest. On the night of the publication party, he dreamed the following:

> I was surrounded by newspapers in many foreign
> languages. However, the headlines were understandable
> to me because they were all the same: "Ataturk is dead,"
> and I was sobbing (Valkan and Yintl 143).[2]

Ataturk represented all the losses Valkan was mourning—his father, his Turkish identity, and his traditions and roots. He says that after completing the book and having this dream, he felt more at home in his chosen country.

Dreams Call Attention to Personal Issues and to Special Memories

It is not unusual for our dreams to use images of the dead to get our attention about personal issues other than the loss of a loved one. Personal issues that existed before the death may surface as a result of grieving. Dreams of this nature appear

---

2 Valkan is with the Washington Psychoanalytic Institute and is on the faculty of the University of Virginia Health Science Center. He is a political psychologist as well as a bereavement therapist. Yintl is an award-winning journalist. In their book, they illustrate how a dream reflects an individual's involvement in mourning (147). They also provide a guide for knowing when the practical end of mourning is reached. This comes when we are able to provide for ourselves something that we were once given by the deceased (38, 40). This is a valuable book for the bereaved.

elsewhere in this book; for example, in one dream a friend's death helped the dreamer with problems regarding his family and the possibility of recurring cancer (chapter 8).

I once heard a military chaplain, speaking to a group of church workers, tell a dream, which he described as vivid, that confirmed that he should become a minister. In this dream he saw his father, who had been a minister, preaching to a crowd. He stood above the elbow-to-elbow crowd, even though he was short, and then he disappeared, as though he were ascending. The dreamer asked, "But what about all these people?" as he thought about who was going to help them now that his father was gone. He heard an abrupt voice say, "You are."

Sometimes dreams bring up experiences from a person's childhood. The following is the dream of a charming older woman. In her letter to me, she was puzzled by her dream about a person with whom she had been in school as a child and who had been dead for a long time. She considered her marriage of many years to George a very good one. But, although she did not say so, perhaps she was often weary of caring for her husband, who was in poor health. Here is her dream:

> I was walking down the street with the first beau I ever
> had. In kindergarten, he kissed me and said, "You're my
> girl and don't go out with anyone else." On my birthday,
> he gave me a diamond ring. As we walked along he
> remarked, "Sophia is dead, George is gone, and I never
> should have married Sophia. It was always you I loved."

In what more beautiful way could a dream say to the dreamer "you are lovable"? And what a nice thing for anyone to hear anytime in life, especially at a time of stress!

Conclusion

My goal in writing this book is to provide evidence that dreaming is a normal part of grieving. I also want to encourage you who mourn to let your dreams help you honor the death as well as the life of your loved one. If your dreams call attention to problems resulting from the loss, you may want to read some books on the subject or share your dreams with a person knowledgeable in psychology and dreams. The variety of books suggested throughout these pages are good sources of information. A person doesn't have to be a professional to be a good listener and offer insights. Still I would agree with ancient Jewish mystics who warn against discussing our dreams with just anyone for fear their significance may be diminished. At the same time, these mystics emphasize that "we should not keep our dreams buried within us" (Hoffman 148).

A long-time friend, Ben Goodwin, MD, brought to my attention the importance of honoring all of life—its sadness, its joy, and the in-between—with the dreaming and dreams that accompany it:

> Be active in your dream work. Look to your own
> meanings—your own associations. Your dreams are
> yours. The symbols are yours. The benefits of integration
> are yours. Honor your dreaming and dreams.

> Honor your caring. Own the sadness of your loss.
> Times of sadness recur. Permit yourself to notice what
> you feel. Attend to your life. Mourning is an important
> phase of caring. Notice it and don't attach yourself to it.
> Enjoy the fullness of life. Dreaming truly helps.

My hope for you is that you will find consolation, guidance, and enhancement of memories in your dreams.

> Blessed are they who mourn, for they will be comforted
> (Mt 5:4).

Appendix:
Keeping a Dream Journal

Most bereaved have not been in the habit of working with their dreams. Their dreams at this time of loss may stand out because they do not usually recall dreams or because their dreams are unusual. Then they may be disturbed by them. My experience is that disturbing dreams become less disturbing when we examine them. Pleasant dreams give us even more enjoyment when we savor them. All dreams enrich our lives and put us in touch with what is going on in our lives—both the inner life and the outer life.

In *Dreams and Spiritual Growth,* Savary, Berne, and Williams compare the world of dreams to a vessel full of precious things. They go on to say that we might make three responses to this vessel full of precious things. We can leave it where we found it and go on our way without examining the contents; we can look at the lovely things and acknowledge them and go on our way; or, we can examine what we find, discover what it means and its value, and put it to work in our lives.

For those who would like to begin taking advantage of the valuable resource of their dreams, keeping a record of your dreams is a starting place, a taking out of the lovely things—and some things that may not seem so lovely at first glance. Just keeping a record may lead you to discover some meaning and will do much to help you appreciate your dreams.

I suggest keeping a record of all your dreams after the death of a close relative or friend for at least a year. All dreams after the death of a significant person may relate in some way to the loss. You will be surprised at how they will help you to cope with your sadness and to resolve other issues that come to your attention because of your loss. Recording your dreams in a journal in memory of the departed loved one is a good way to honor both your loved one and your dreams.

The organization of your journal can help you examine what you find in your dream and go a long way toward helping you find the meaning and value of it. Caution: If you let the writing and organizing of your dreams become a chore you might be tempted to drop it all together or not be able to do justice to any of them. In *Dreams That Can Change Your Life*, Alan Siegel reminds us that "one dream explored in depth is more valuable than a month's worth of dreams that remain untouched and invisible in your journal" (267). But keeping a record of all your dreams gives you the advantage of reviewing a series of dreams. The dreams before or after a dream may provide understanding to the dream to which you are giving attention.

A loose-leaf notebook is practical to use for a dream journal. That way, you can add pages with notes and comments about the dream at a later time when you have had more time to reflect on the dream. In a blank book you would have to leave space after the dream. A good way to use a blank book is to make rough notes of your dream and your work on it, then record them in permanent form later. One of the attractive blank books you find in bookstores would make a lovely book for recording your dreams and grief experience.

The format I use in recording my dreams is basically what I learned from Dr. Gayle Delaney. It is discussed in detail in her books *Living Your Dreams* and *Breakthrough Dreaming*. Here are the items I include for each dream:

- **Daynotes:** In anticipation of a dream, make notes in the evening of feelings, events, and people that have been a part of your day. Three or four lines should be plenty. If you forget or don't have time, fill this in after your dream. These notes will jog your memory about what has been going on and will be extremely helpful when you refer to a dream days and even years later.

- **Date:** Recording the date of each dream is important for later reference.

- **Title:** Leave a space and come back to this.

- **The Dream:** Record your dream as soon as possible because all but the most extraordinary tend to fade rapidly.

- **Commentary:** Thoughts and feelings you have the moment you awaken as well as association with the events of yesterday should be recorded. A title may come to mind or you might want to create a title at this point. A title will help you remember and identify your dream quickly when you re-read your journal.

Now you are ready to look at the elements of your dream. This may be done later when you have the time. Usually I have to reflect on my dreams off and on over a period of time. Elements of the dream you want to look at are settings, people, objects, feelings, and action. Here you need to be careful to remember that the meaning of your dream image is special to you and can only be understood in the context of your experience. A dream dictionary is not too helpful because it does not take into account the dreamer's experience with the image.

This book cannot include techniques for understanding the elements of your dream. However, you will gain some meaning from and much appreciation for your dreams by recording them. Developing the habit of giving attention to your dreams will aid your understanding of them.

There are a variety of ways to organize a dream journal. The important thing is to preserve the dream's moods, images, and scenes until we can reflect on it more fully. Montague Ullman and Nan Zimmerman as well as others are strong on this viewpoint. The four books listed below offer methods for recording dreams:

- *Breakthrough Dreaming* by Gayle Delaney (19-22)

- *The Dream Game* by Ann Faraday (37-48)

- *Working with Dreams* by Ullman and Zimmerman (112-15)

- *Dreams That Can Change Your Life* by Alan Siegel (267-69)

These books also give techniques for working with dreams. Even using these techniques, you cannot always understand your grief dreams; nevertheless, you should work with them using the techniques of your choice because meaning cannot usually be determined until you do. In this book I have tried to demonstrate other ways of getting at the meaning, such as looking at the circumstances of one's life at the time of dreaming. Some dreams are very simple to understand. Others remain mysterious.

You have probably already recalled a dream or you would not be reading this. Do not fret if you do not recall additional dreams. Recalling dreams is not always a part of grieving. If you start a journal with a dream and no more are recalled, you still have a journal of your time of mourning with the daynote entries.

A Page from My Dream Journal

Daynotes (written the evening before): My husband, Bill, and I have just returned to Louisville after a year in California to move to Ft. Worth, Texas. He has been retired one year, but this evening we have attended a banquet for graduate students because the last of his students are graduating. I thought the speaker was lengthy and dry. I am tired.

Date: May 17, 1996

Title: Squiggles in the Sky

Dream: I'm outside of a vacated brick building. Plants at the corners of the foundation are drying up. I'm trudging wearily back and forth carrying water to them to keep them alive. The sky is dark so I guess it is nighttime—or it may just be cloudy. While I'm watering the plants, I'm startled by white squiggles beginning to appear in the sky. Friends, Betty and Ed, appear and watch. After a long time I finish watering the plants and the squiggles have filled the sky. We've never seen anything like this. I wake up wondering at the meaning of such an image.

Commentary: The building in this dream is institutional-like with no activity. This describes the institution with which my husband has been associated. With a change in administration, most professors who were there when we first went there have retired or been paid to resign. There are two-thirds less students. My husband managed to stay until retirement age but doesn't think he can remain in the same city in such a stressful atmosphere. I feel tired and sad. I don't want to think about moving. Betty and Ed are not moving. They have found ways to be content and remain. Why can't we? The expression "handwriting on the wall" (from Daniel 5) comes to mind in connection with the calligraphy-like squiggles in the sky. This term is used sometimes to say that it is time to do a particular thing one does not really want to do; sometimes it means "fate"; and other times it is a warning. Perhaps this dream is telling me that the situation I'm in is my fate, the way things are in my life. Then again maybe the squiggles are like silver linings to clouds and are promising me better times. Maybe both.

Notes: I notice that in doing the commentary, I have looked at the elements (setting, people, objects, and feelings) and gathered meaning from them. This does not always happen. Usually further work is required. What remains for me to do is to put the insight to work in my life. That is, accept the inevitable move with the expectation of a silver lining (better times).

Works Cited
and Recommended

Aleixandre, Vicente. "My Grandfather's Death." In *Selected Poems of Vicente Aleixandre,* edited by Lewis Hyde and translated by Stephen Kessler. New York: Harper and Row, n.d. Cited in Moffat 87-88.

Berggolts, Olga. "Infidelity." Translated by Dan Weissbort. In *Post-War Russian Poetry,* edited by Dan Weissbort. New York: Penguin Books, 1974. Quoted in Moffat 209-10.

Boorstin, Daniel J. *The Creators.* New York: Random House, 1992.

Bosnak, Robert. *A Little Course in Dreams.* Boston: Shambhala, 1988.

Bownas, Geoffrey, and Anthony Thwaite, trans. "On the Death of Emperor Tenji." In *The Penguin Book of Japanese Verse.* New York: Penguin Books, 1964.

Brooks, Anne M. *The Grieving Time.* Garden City, New York: Dial Press, 1985.

Brothers, Joyce. *Widowed.* New York: Simon & Schuster, 1990.

Brown, Eugene M., ed. *Dreams, Visions, and Prophecies of Don Bosco.* New Rochelle, New York: Don Bosco Publications, Inc., 1986.

Brown, Rodney Paul. "Possible Precognitive Dreams of My Father's Unexpected Death." *Association for the Study of Dreams Newsletter* 4, no. 1 (Feb. 1987): 11-12.

Bryant, Judy, Leslie Scanlon, and Grace Schneider. "The Families." *The Courier-Journal,* Louisville (14 Sept. 1990): A1, A6.

Burham, Sophy. *A Book of Angels.* New York: Ballantine Books, 1990.

Callaway, H. *The Religious System of the Amazulu.* London: Trubner and Co., 1868. Quoted in Hayashida, "Significance of Dreams," 83-4.

Cliff, Jean, and Wallace Cliff. *The Hero Journey in Dreams.* New York: Crossroads. 1988.

Craighead, Meinrad. *The Mother Songs.* New York: Paulist Press, 1986.

Davidson, Glen W. *Living with Dying.* Minneapolis: Augsburg Publishing House, 1975.

Delaney, Gayle. *Breakthrough Dreaming.* New York: Bantam Books, 1991.

———. "Joyful Dreams." *Association for the Study of Dreams Newsletter* 3, no. 3 (Sept. 1986): 1.

———. *Living Your Dreams.* San Francisco: Harper and Row, 1981.

Dickens, Charles. *Dombey and Son.* Oxford: University Press, 1950.

Duncan, Denis, ed. *Meditations by J. B. Phillips for This Day.* Waco: Word Books, 1974.

Evans, Christopher, ed., completed by Peter Evans. *Landscapes of the Night.* New York: Viking Press, 1984.

Faraday, Ann. *The Dream Game.* New York: Harper and Row, 1974.

Fishel, Elizabeth. *Sisters.* New York: Bantam Books [William Morrow], 1979.

Gendlin, Eugene T. *Let Your Body Interpret Your Dreams.* Wilmette, Illinois: Chiron, 1986.

George, Phil. "The Visit." In *Voices of the Rainbow: Contemporary Poetry by American Indians,* edited by Kenneth Rosen. New York: Viking Press, 1975. Cited in Moffat 203.

Gerne, Margarete. *Association for the Study of Dreams Newsletter* 6, no. 2 (March/April 1986): 1-2.

Gollnick, James. *Dreams in the Psychology of Religion.* Lewiston, New York: Edwin Mellen Press, 1987.

Goodison, Lucy. *The Dreams of Women.* New York: Norton, 1995.

Grotjahn, Martin. "The Dream in Analytic Group Therapy." In *The Dream in Clinical Practice.* Edited by Joseph M. Natterson. New York: Jason Aronson, 1980.

Guiley, Rosemary Ellen. *The Encyclopedia of Dreams: Symbols and Interpretations.* New York: Crossroads, 1993.

Hall, C. Ray. "A Legacy of Loss." *The Courier-Journal,* Louisville (31 July 1994): H1.

Halligan, Frederica B., and John J. Shea. "Sacred Images in Dreamwork." *Pastoral Psychology* 40, no. 1 (Sept. 1991): 25-38.

Hayashida, Nelson Osamer. "The Significance of Dreams and Visions Among Members of the Baptist Churches of Zambia with Special Reference to the Manyika Baptist Association and to Selected Urban Areas," Ph.D. diss., University of Edinburgh, 1993.

—————. "Dreams: A Way of Revelation for the African Church." *The Commission* 53, no. 1 (Jan. 1990): 60-61.

Hendricks, Lois Lindsey. *Discovering My Biblical Dream Heritage.* San Jose: Resource Publications, 1989.

Hoffman, Edward. *The Way of Splendor: Jewish Mysticism and Modern Psychology.* Boulder: Shambhala, 1981.

Ivey, Sara. "When I Found My Sister, I Found Myself." *Woman's Day* (16 Jan. 1990): 70, 72-3, 84-5.

Jaffe, Aniela. *Spring.* New York: Analytical Psychology Club, 1959. Quoted in *The Meaning in Dreams and Dreaming,* Maria F. Mahoney. New York: Citadel Press, 1966.

Johnson. Rheta Grimsley. "Sisters Are Like Shadows of Our Other Selves." *The Commercial Appeal* (18 Sept. 1991): A9.

Kast, Verena. *A Time to Mourn.* Einsiedeln, Switzerland: Daimon Verlag, 1988.

Kelsey, Morton. *Christo-Psychology.* New York: Crossroads, 1982.

—————. Foreword ("The Dream As Religious Experience") to *Dreams, Visions, and Prophecies of Don Bosco,* edited by Eugene M. Brown.

—————. *Reaching: The Journey to Fulfillment.* San Francisco: Harper and Row, 1989.

Kepler, Thomas S., ed. *The Journal of John Woolman.* Cleveland: World Publishing, 1954.

Kikaku. In *One Hundred Famous Haiku,* translated by Daniel C. Buchanan. Tokyo: Japan Pub., 1973.

—————. In *Haiku Harvest,* translated by Peter Beilenson and Harry Behn. Mount Vernon, New York: Peter Pauper Press, 1962.

Kornbluth, Jesse. "Victory Over the Klan." *The Courier-Journal,* Louisville (8 Nov. 1987): D5.

Kutner, Lawrence M. "Regeneration: Sibling Relationships Shift When Parents Die." *The Courier-Journal,* Louisville (14 April 1990): H4.

Lemoyne, Giovanni Battista, SDB, et al. *The Biographical Memoirs of Saint John Bosco.* Vols. 1- . Translated by Diego Borgatello, SDB. New Rochelle, New York: Salesiana Publishers, 1964- .

Lewis, C. S. *A Grief Observed.* New York: Bantam Books, 1961.

Loewald, Hans. "The Waning of the Oedipus Complex." *Journal of the American Psychoanalytic Association* 27, no. 4 (1979).

Machado, Antonio. *The Dream Below the Sun: Selected Poems of Antonio Machado.* Translated by Willis Barnstone. Trumansburg, New York: The Crossing Press, 1981.

Mahoney, Maria F. *The Meaning in Dreams and Dreaming.* New York: Citadel Press, 1966.

Marshall, Catherine. *Something More.* New York: Avon Books, 1974.

Marty, Martin E. *A Cry of Absence.* San Francisco: Harper and Row, 1983.

———. *Friendship.* Allen, Texas: Argus Communications, 1980.

McDonald, Phoebe. *Dreams: Night Language of the Soul."* New York: Continuum, 1987.

Miller, William McElwee. "Khadijeh, Dreamer and Poetess." In *Ten Muslims Meet Christ.* Grand Rapids, Michigan: Eerdmans, 1969.

Milton, John. "Methought I Saw." In *Paradise Regained: The Minor Poems and "Samson Agonistes."* Edited by Merritt Y. Hughes. New York: Odyssey Press, 1937.

Moffat, Mary Jane, ed. *In the Midst of Winter: Selections from the Literature of Mourning.* New York: Random House, 1982.

Moody, John H. "Dreaming and Bereavement." *Pastoral Psychology* 16, no. 1 (Fall 1973): 11-12.

Mushindo, Paul Bwembya. *The Life of a Zambian Evangelist.* University of Zambia: Institute for African Studies, 1973. Quoted in Hayashida.

Nieburg, Herbert, and Arlene Fisher. *Pet Loss.* New York: Harper and Row, 1982.

Oates, Wayne E. *Pastoral Care and Counseling in Grief and Separation.* Philadelphia: Fortress Press, 1976.

Parkes, Colin Murray. *Bereavement: Studies of Grief in Adult Life.* New York: International University Press, 1972.

———. "The First Year of Bereavement." In *Psychiatry* 33 (1970): 465.

Pastan, Linda. *The Five Stages of Grief.* New York: Norton, 1966. Quoted in Moffat 255-7.

Proust, Marcel. *Letters of Marcel Proust.* Edited and translated by Mina K. Curtiss. New York: Random House, 1949.

Quakenbush, Jamie, and Denise Graveline. *When Your Pet Dies.* New York: Simon and Schuster, 1985.

Rando, Therese. *Grieving: How to Go on Living When Someone You Love Dies.* Lexington, Massachusetts: Lexington Books, 1988.

Sanford, John. *Dreams: God's Forgotten Language*. Philadelphia: J. B. Lippincott, 1968.

Sarton, May. "All Souls." In *Collected Poems, 1930-1973*. New York: Norton, 1974. Quoted in Moffat 271.

Savary, Louis M., Patricia H. Berne, and Strephon Kaplan Williams. *Dreams and Spiritual Growth: A Christian Approach to Dreamwork*. New York: Paulist Press, 1984.

Siegel, Alan B. *Dreams That Can Change Your Life*. Los Angeles: Jeremy P. Tarcher, 1990.

Siegel, Bernie S. *Peace, Love and Healing*. New York: Harper and Row, 1989.

Ullman, Montague, and Nan Zimmerman. *Working with Dreams*. New York: Dell, 1979.

Valkan, Vamik D., and Elizabeth Yintl. *Life After Loss: The Lessons of Grief*. New York: Charles Scribner's Sons, 1993.

Viorst, Judith. *Necessary Losses*. New York: Simon and Schuster, 1986.

von Franz, Marie-Louise. *On Dreams and Death,* translated by Emmanuel Xipolitas Kennedy and Vernon Brooks. Boston: Shambhala, 1987.

Wilson, Edmund. *The Thirties*. Edited by Leon Edel. New York: Farrar, Straus and Giroux, 1980.

Yuan, P' An. "In Mourning for His Dead Wife." In *Love and the Turning Year: One Hundred More Poems from the Chinese*, edited by Kenneth Rexroth. New York: New Directions, 1970.

Zimmerman, Nan. "After the Dream Is Over." In *The Variety of Dream Experiences*, edited by Montague Ullman and Claire Limmer. New York: Continuum, 1987.

Index

Index

Facing Adversity

RISING ABOVE
A Guide to Overcoming Obstacles and Finding Happiness

Jerry Wilde, Ph.D.

Paper, 144 pages, 5½" x 8½", ISBN: 0-89390-345-0

Everyone experiences some setbacks, losses, or health problems. Such events can be opportunities for growth. Pain can be a good friend asking you to change. This book by a psychologist who had to face his own life-threatening disease, lays out some tools that will help you face any dilemma with a minimum of suffering. Great referral book for counselors.

THE CURE
The Hero's Journey with Cancer

G. Frank Lawlis, Ph.D.

Paper, 64 Pages, 5½" x 8½", ISBN: 0-89390-273-X

Caregiver's kit (book, 2 audiocassettes, caregiver's guide)

G. Frank Lawlis developed this fable — about a wolf who consults other animals for a cure for a mysterious disease — as a way to help people with cancer confront their fears. The Caregiver's Kit includes the book itself, a 56-page caregiver's guide, and two audiocassettes containing instructions and guided meditations.

WHEN YOUR LONG-TERM MARRIAGE ENDS
A Workbook for Divorced Women

Elaine Newell

Paper, 144 pages, 6" x 9", ISBN: 0-89390-291-8

When Your Long-Term Marriage Ends is a workbook written especially for the woman who finds herself facing the challenging transition of a divorce. This book leads the reader through the stages of panic, rejection, anger, loneliness, awareness, responsibility, and, finally, forgiveness.

Call Toll-Free 1-888-273-7782 for current prices.
See last page for ordering information.

Personal Growth

BALANCING YOUR LIFE
Setting Personal Goals

Paul Stevens

Paper, 96 pages, 4¼" x 7", ISBN: 0-89390-375-2

The key to improving your life, according to noted "worklife" expert Paul Stevens, is planning. All you need is privacy, peace and quiet, a pad of paper, and lots of enthusiasm. *Balancing Your Life: Setting Personal Goals* provides that extra push. It will help you sort through the conflicting issues you deal with each day, the opportunities you want to explore, and the actions you need to take to bring balance to your life. In the end, you'll emerge with a set of clear personal goals that help you balance career with the rest of your life.

WRITING YOUR WAY TO WHOLENESS
Creative Exercises for Personal Growth

Terre Ouwehand

Paper, 220 pages, 6" x 9", ISBN: 0-89390-312-4

Are you trying to grow spiritually? If you are a budding writer — or you just enjoy journalizing — here's good news. Terre Ouwehand uncovers the link between your most casual writing and your spiritual growth. Select from hundreds of exercises to uncover your creativity and discover your real feelings. Writing and soulwork has never been so much fun.

SO, WHAT IS ASSERTIVENESS?
An Assertiveness Training Course

Chrissie Whitehead

Paper, 64 pages, 8½" x 11", ISBN: 0-89390-296-9

Aggressive vs. assertive. What's the difference? This book clarifies the difference between assertive and aggressive behavior, emphasizing that assertive behavior brings about acceptable results to all involved. You'll appreciate the easy-to-use lesson plans and photocopiable handouts which lead to identifying and changing patterns of aggressive behavior. And you'll like the author's ideas for setting up and promoting the course, too. The lessons can be taught as a separate course, worked into a self-esteem or life-skills course, or they can be used in less structured situations in youth or neighborhood groups, teacher in-service, adult education programs or business offices.

Call Toll-Free 1-888-273-7782 for current prices.
See last page for ordering information.

Dealing with Loss

GRIEF MINISTRY
Helping Others Mourn
Donna Reilly Williams & JoAnn Sturzl
Paper, 195 pages, 5½" x 8½", ISBN: 0-89390-233-0

GRIEF MINISTRY
Facilitator's Guide
JoAnn Sturzl & Donna Reilly Williams
Paper, 144 perforated pages, 8½" x 11", ISBN: 0-89390-227-6

G*rief Ministry: Helping Others Mourn* fills the need for an up-to-date resource that combines spiritual and psychological insights about griefwork. It covers general aspects of grieving, empathy, communication, listening, and prayer. The authors share insights on handling difficult situations, including such special cases as suicide, the death of a baby, job loss, AIDS, and divorce.

The *Facilitator's Guide* shows how to set up a program to train grief ministers using *Grief Ministry: Helping Others Mourn* as a textbook. The guide includes group listening and role-playing exercises, scenarios for discussion, a resource listing, and useful handouts with photocopy permission included.

HEALING OUR LOSSES
A Journal for Working Through Your Grief
Jack Miller, Ph.D.
Paper, 104 pages, 7" x 10", ISBN: 0-89390-255-1

In *Healing Our Losses*, the author shares experiences of loss in his own life and will guide you to record your memories, thoughts, and feelings, about loss in your life. Journaling may be done alone by an individual or in a group setting.

Order from your local bookseller, or contact:

 Resource Publications, Inc.
160 E. Virginia Street #290
San Jose, CA 95112-5876
1-408-286-8505
1-408-287-8748(FAX)
1-888-273-7782(TOLL FREE)
www.rpinet.com
orders@rpinet.com

SG